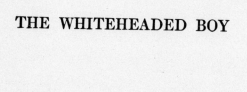

THE WHITEHEADED BOY

THE
WHITEHEADED BOY

A COMEDY IN THREE ACTS

BY
LENNOX ROBINSON

WITH AN INTRODUCTION BY
ERNEST BOYD

G. P. PUTNAM'S SONS
NEW YORK AND LONDON
The Knickerbocker Press

To

"AUNT ELLEN"

INTRODUCTION

A chapter in the history of the Irish Theatre
was closed in 1907, when *The Playboy of the
Western World* was produced, bringing in its
train notoriety, fame and a relative degree of
popular success. The recognition of the genius
of J. M. Synge was the culminating point in
the movement for the creation of a national
folk-drama which he had initiated in the
company of Lady Gregory, Padraic Colum and
William Boyle. These were the pioneers of
the peasant play and each contributed a definite
element to that type of drama, marking the lim-
itations within which it was to develop. As a
result of the enhanced prestige of the Theatre
and of the extension of its influence, a great
number of new playwrights came forward,
including several whose names were to attain
a prominence which has obscured the prior
claims of their predecessors, the dramatists,
who laid the foundations of the success enjoyed
by the Abbey Theatre after the death of Synge
in 1909. A convention had been created and
it was not long before a host of peasant melo-
dramatists arose to fulfil the demand for such

plays. What was obvious in the verbal exuberance of Synge, in the profound realism of Padraic Colum, in the drollery of Lady Gregory, could be imitated, and popular folk-drama came to be manufactured according to a formula.

One of the young men who at that time was influenced by seeing the performances of the Irish Players was the author of *The White-headed Boy.* Mr. Lennox Robinson is the son of a clergyman and was born in Cork in 1886. He was one of a group of writers in that city who have in recent years given to Irish literature some of its best work. His own plays and the novels of Mr. Daniel Corkery have already been acclaimed beyond the borders of Ireland. But back in the days of the Synge controversies the theatre was the chief preoccupation of that circle to which the Abbey Theatre now owes many of the most successful and some of the best, plays in its repertory; among others, *Birthright,* by T. C. Murray, and *The Yellow Bittern,* by Daniel Corkery. They had founded a local organization for the production of their work and one, at least, of Mr. Robinson's 'prentice efforts was staged there, but has never been published or otherwise acknowledged by him. It is called *The Lesson of Life* and the very title suggests reasons for the author's discretion. Indeed, he himself has been the sharpest critic of his early writings, and is not disposed to take very seriously even the first of his plays to be accepted by the Abbey Theatre. In the order of their production these were *The Clancy Name* (1908), *The Cross Roads* (1909) and *Harvest* (1910).

It is doubtless unkind to dwell upon the early experiments of a writer who more or less disowns them, but apart from the perfectly legitimate interest which such things have for the critic, the remarkable development of Lennox Robinson's gift for the theatre is nowhere more effectively shown than in the contrast between those three plays and the maturer work which has been crowned with the great and deserved success of *The Whiteheaded Boy.* In the little one-act play, *The Clancy Name,* merits are discernible which are not so apparent in either of the more ambitious pieces which followed it. The conflict arises between a mother, whose pride of race is the passion of her life, and her son, whose sense of duty compels him to confess that he is guilty of a crime to the authorities who do not suspect him. She tries to prevent him from bringing disgrace on the family name, but the young man resists the appeal and goes off to give himself up. By the device of having him killed while trying to rescue a child from being trampled by a runaway horse, the dramatist solves too easily the problem which he had presented with convincing force.

The Cross Roads, however, was such a denial of all coherence and probability that the question of the element of inevitability, essential to tragedy, simply did not arise. Having postulated a loveless marriage between an ambitious, educated country girl and an impossibly brutal farmer, the author asks us to believe that this puts a curse upon the farm. The poultry refuse to lay eggs, the cattle die, even the fertilizer goes on strike, and we are shown a ghastly picture of the physical and moral deterioration of the household, terminating with the exit of the husband, who announces that he is "going down the road for a sup of drink" and "God help you when I come back." Not even the fine acting of Miss Sara Allgood could save this from being the *reductio ad absurdum* of the peasant melodrama. Almost the same can be said of *Harvest,* except that the theme itself is inherently sound, and need not have degenerated into the banalities of Brieux's *Blanchette,* with its commonplace variant of the girl who took the wrong turning. Mr. Robinson's subject is that of the problems raised by the extension of educational facilities to people whose peculiar needs and opportunities are not considered by those who draw up the syllabus. The application of this theme to Irish conditions would have provided excellent material for a dramatist knowing rural Ireland, but here the subject is frittered away into a lurid tale of seduction, in which the heroine discourses in the traditional manner of melodrama. Miss Maire O'Neill's art could not conceal the essential unreality of the words she spoke so beautifully. But these three plays of his nonage were merely the experiments of a dramatist who was learning his craft, and who differs, in this respect, from some of his contemporaries who have had only one play to give to the Irish Theatre, and whose reputations rest on that first play, apparently free from all critical scrutiny. Lennox Robinson's work is a record of progress, whose turning point was in 1912, when his *Patriots* was produced.

The subject of that drama is one which, in the retrospect of recent tragic years in Ireland, takes on a peculiar interest, for it was nothing less than a dramatisation of the crisis in Irish political thought whose ultimate expression is the Sinn Fein movement of to-day. The central figure of *Patriots* is an old rebel who comes back after years of imprisonment to find that other men and other methods are in favor with those who control the nationalist fight. In James Nugent's day physical force was the weapon, but the new generation seems wholly absorbed in parliamentary methods, and regards his insurrectionary faith as merely an obsolete relic of the romantic period. Mr. Robinson draws an exceedingly faithful and

vivid picture of the state of Irish politics at
that time, when the ardor of revolution appeared to have died, and the constitutional
Home Rule Party's authority and prestige were
supreme. There is a real tragedy in the defeat
and dismay of the revolutionary man of action
when he is compelled to make way for leaders
who are ignorant of all that was the glory of
his youth, and who can prove by logic that his
methods are useless. In a poem of poignant
eloquence, W. B. Yeats brooded over that same
mood in which *Patriots* was conceived, when
he wrote:

> Yet they were of a different kind
> The names that stilled your childish play,
> They have gone about the world like wind,
> But little time they had to pray
> For whom the hangman's rope was spun,
> And what, God help us, could they save:
> Romantic Ireland's dead and gone,
> It's with O'Leary in the grave.

The revolt, at that time barely perceptible,
against the prevailing apathy of the national
spirit, flared up a few years later in the Sinn
Fein insurrection of 1916 and the complete
overthrow of the existing political order, whose
success was postulated by the dramatist. But
political prophecy is not an essential part of a
good play.

INTRODUCTION

Just one year before that Easter Rising in Dublin, Mr. Robinson returned to the same theme, in another of its aspects. *The Dreamers* is an historical play which treats of the last chapter in the life of Robert Emmet, the ill-fated leader of the abortive insurrection which was the aftermath of the Irish Rebellion of 1798. The author's purpose is to show this tragic figure as the victim of the shiftlessness and dishonest futility of his followers. He has always been more fortunate than Synge when he has drawn pictures of the Irish character which did not coincide with the illusions of sentimental patriotism. Just as *Harvest* escaped even the censure of the hypersensitive who hooted *The Playboy of the Western World,* when both were presented by the Irish Players during their visit to America in 1911, so *The Dreamers* was well received by audiences in which there must have been many who were actually preparing to face the same death as Robert Emmet in 1916.

It was at the close of that year that *The Whiteheaded Boy* had its première at the Abbey Theatre, where it at once enjoyed the success and appreciation which were confirmed when it was subsequently produced in London. Miss Maire O'Neill, who, like so many of the original group of the Irish Players, had left the theatre, returned for this occasion and created the delightful part of Aunt Ellen, one of the finest comedy characters on the modern stage. Subsequently, when she repeated the part in London she was supported by Miss Sara Allgood, Mr. Arthur Sinclair and others belonging to the group of Players who first made the Irish Theatre famous. The strength of this play undoubtedly lies in the perfect combination of form and content, and the natural, unstrained drollery of speech combined with a subject which develops realistically and logically, yet whose humor is that of cumulative effect. There is not a deliberately manufactured phrase in it, not one situation that is forced and stagey, for the whole comedy arises out of the relations which inevitably establish themselves between the characters. An attractive innovation, too, is the narrative form of the stage directions, which in the printed text enable the reader to have the illusion of listening to a living commentary. After the telegraphic jargon of the conventional stage direction, and the garrulous dissertations of Bernard Shaw, Mr. Robinson's method is pleasing and original. "Kate's off to the kitchen now. Aren't I after telling you she's a great help to her mother!" Even between brackets this is preferable to "Exit Kate, L. U. E.," or words to that effect.

Before writing *The Whiteheaded Boy,* Lennox Robinson had been at work upon a novel which was in the publishers' hands in Dublin when the Easter Rising took place, but the manuscript was destroyed in the bombardment of the city. When *A Young Man from the South* eventually appeared, its singular appropriateness to the occasion was apparent, for it is a study of the evolution of a young Irishman from loyal Unionism to passionate nationalism. The protagonist is drawn from the life of a Southern Irish city like that in which the author's own youth was passed. He comes to Dublin and is gradually converted to a belief in the national identity of his country, so that Mr. Robinson has many opportunities of describing the various social and intellectual groups which go to the making of that fascinating city. The publication of this book coincided with that of several novels purporting to describe the condition of Ireland during the years of Sinn Fein, but few have the dispassionate reality of Mr. Robinson's. Although a careful and sympathetic observer, he was not a partisan, and neither indulged a malevolent spleen against the nationalist enthusiasts nor romanticised the facts. His humor plays equally with the naïvetés of what is known as "Irish Ireland" and the pretentions of its counterpart "West Britain." Although after the insurrection, he had actually to re-write the story, he scrupulously refrained from making copy out of the living and the dead who participated in that adventure. The temptation to do so was strong, because it had been 'done by one of his contemporaries in a novel which was published at the same time, and it would have provided a natural dénouement to his story. But in a foreword he explained his scruples. "The combining of real events with imaginary persons seemed likely to lead readers to combine real persons with imaginary events in the book, a result which would offend the living and be unjust to the dead." Thus this work, which is an imaginative reconstruction of what others reported photographically, was deprived by the author's delicacy of a powerful extraneous aid to popular success.

Since *The Whiteheaded Boy* Mr. Robinson has given *The Lost Leader* to the Irish Theatre and has published another volume of fiction, *Eight Short Stories*. In the former he makes the daring experiment of writing a play based upon the popular Irish superstition that Parnell is not dead, but living in obscurity, and he actually sets him upon the stage to face the situation of an Ireland whose policy is Sinn Fein. In the latter work he has collected a sheaf of sketches of contemporary life, with some successful ventures into the realm of the supernatural, which indicate that his craftsmanship in fiction is advancing as surely as in the theatre. For the rest, his life is crowded with activities without being eventful, a rare circumstance in Ireland! He is immersed in the work of building up Irish rural libraries, which is being carried out under the auspices of the Carnegie Trust. Nevertheless, he has never lost his active interest in the Irish Theatre.

In the autumn of 1918 he made an effort to supplement the scope of the Abbey Theatre by launching, with the coöperation of W. B. Yeats, James Stephens and myself, the Dublin Drama League, which was thus the first institution of the kind in the British Islands. Our desire was to enable plays to be produced of the kind which did not come within the intentions of the Abbey Theatre. During the first year, Mr. Robinson was secretary of the League and gave his services as producer, with the result that a successful series of Continental and other plays were given in Dublin for the first time. Then he became, for the second time in his career, manager of the Abbey Theatre and pulled it out of the rut into which it had subsided after the Players began to disperse and their substitutes had not yet found their feet. This excellent process of rehabilitation was unfortunately checked during the last year by the restrictions of the military curfew law, which put even the most prosperous commercial theatres to great losses. But since the armistice hope is revived and Mr. Robinson is courageously announcing his determination to begin all over again, for now it will be necessary to form a new company of players and to train them in the traditions of the Theatre. Of the best that has been created in those traditions *The Whiteheaded Boy* is an example, and Lennox Robinson deserves well of all who have a care for the Irish Theatre. At the outset of that brave undertaking W. B. Yeats's aim was to secure an audience for "the half dozen minds who are likely to be the dramatic imagination of Ireland for this generation." The author of this play has obviously established his claim to be counted amongst that number.

Ernest Boyd.

New York, September, 1921.

PREFACE

In its conception, *The Whiteheaded Boy* was to have been full of symbolic meaning; worse than that, it was to have been full of political meaning. Once, when I was very young, I wrote a violent play called *The Cross Roads,* the chief characters in which were a wife full of idealism and a brutal husband. A critic professed to read into my play a meaning which I had never dreamed of and accused me of writing a political tract on the eternal subject of Celt and Saxon. I scoffed at the accusation but I did not forget it and, years afterwards, I conceived the idea of displaying the British Empire in the form of a large, overgrown family kept together, more or less against its will, by an illogical, absurd, generous, scheming, lovable mother. I made Ireland her youngest child, half black sheep, half mother's darling (or, as we say here, "whiteheaded boy"). He was to be spoiled and petted, bullied and slapped, given too many sweets one day and shut up in the attic on a diet of bread and water the next, praised and blamed and left finally so bewildered and bemused that the only definite idea left to him is that of cutting himself free from his impossible family and making his own life in his own way. Great Britain itself (to which I gave the obviously appropriate name of George) was to be the member of the family most deserving of our pity, overburdened with responsibilities, "pulled this way and that way. Look at the life I've led between you all and no one thinking that maybe I'd want to get married or have a bit of fun or spend a bit of money. . . ." Somehow, that bit of symbolism has remained and in George (at any rate as Mr. Sydney Morgan so beautifully plays him) I do still see poor harassed England, full of futile rages and firm decisions followed immediately by weak compromises, an England which would prefer above all things to be free of responsibilities with leisure and money to enjoy itself.

But apart from George and a speech in the third act which now rings a little false all the symbolism has disappeared. That the note of this speech is untrue to the key of the play is the clearest proof of how completely it *has* disappeared. It started to disappear the moment I put pen to paper. Like the Mr. Edwards who tried to be a philosopher "cheerfulness was always breaking in." Aunt Ellen, in fact, kept breaking in, and Mr. Duffy. They, in my conception, were to play a very small part in the parable. But though it is comparatively easy to beget children, once born they are hard to control and when I started to write the Geoghegans and the Duffys took the bit between their teeth and for a fortnight drove my pen exactly in the direction they wanted it to go. By that time *The Whiteheaded Boy* was finished and, reading it over, I had ruefully to admit that it was not the play I had set out to write. But on the whole I was not displeased, for few people are interested in the relations between Ireland and England but the problem of the whiteheaded boy is vital from Ballycolman to the world's end.

I suppose it is mad of me to make this confession. I can never expect to be taken seriously as a dramatist now that I have admitted to such a haphazard, uncontrolled method of work. Professor Baker will hold me up as a warning, not as an example, to his class at Harvard. I can't say that I shall not mind that. I shall. But I shall mind much more if a hasty critic skims this preface, catches sight of the words "symbolism" and "politics," and proceeds to describe *The Whiteheaded Boy* as a political tract disguised as a play. It isn't, indeed it isn't. I haven't the remotest idea what it means politically.

LENNOX ROBINSON.

Ireland,
June, 1921

THE WHITEHEADED BOY

Produced by Charles Dillingham at Henry Miller's Theatre, New York, October 17, 1921, with the following cast:

MRS. GEOGHEGAN . . . . *Maureen Delany*
GEORGE . . ⎫ . . . . *Sydney Morgan*
PETER . . . ⎪ . . *Harry Hutchinson*
KATE . . . ⎬ her children . . . . . *Norah Desmond*
JANE . . . . ⎪ . *Suzanne McKernan*
BABY . . . . ⎪ . . . . . *May Fitzgerald*
DENIS . . . ⎭ . . . . . *Arthur Shields*
DONOUGH BROSNAN (engaged to Jane)
                            J. A. O'Rourke
JOHN DUFFY (Chairman,
    Rural District Council) . . . . *Arthur Sinclair*
DELIA (his daughter, engaged to Denis)
                            Gertrude Murphy
HANNAH (a servant) . . . . . . *Christine Hayden*
AUNT ELLEN . . . . *Maire O'Neill*

THE WHITEHEADED BOY

Act I

[MRS. GEOGHEGAN'S *house is at the head of the street, facing the priest's house; the shop is at the other end of the village, between* MICHAEL BROSNAN'S *public-house and* DUFFY'S *yard.* WILLIAM GEOGHEGAN (*God rest his soul*) *was a very genteel man, and when the wife brought him the house and the bit of land instead of getting a tenant for it like a sensible man (and the whole village knew* CLANCY, *the vet., was mad to take it) nothing would do him but live in it himself and walk down to his business every day like a millionaire. 'Tis too high notions poor* WILLIAM *always had—and his sister,* ELLEN, *worse again than himself, craning after anything new she'd be like a cow through a fence—but, indeed,* WILLIAM'S *notions didn't stand too well to him, and when he died he left his fam-*

3

*ily—six of them, no less—in a poor
enough way. But the eldest boy—*GEORGE
*—was always terrible industrious, and he
made two of himself after the father
died, and they managed to pull along.
You can see from the appearance of the
room we're looking at they're not wanting
for comfort.* MRS. GEOGHEGAN—*poor*
WILLIAM'S *widow (that's her behind the
table setting out the cups)—is a hearty
woman yet, and, after all, I suppose she's
not more than sixty-five years of age. A
great manager she is, and, indeed, she'd
need to be with three unmarried daughters under her feet all day and two big
men of sons. You'd not like to deny*
MRS. GEOGHEGAN *anything she's such a
pleasant way with her, yet you know she's
not what I'd call a clever woman, I mean
to say she hasn't got the book-knowledge,
the "notions" her husband had or her
sister* ELLEN. *But maybe she's better
without them, sure what good is book-
knowledge to the mother of a family?
She's a simple, decent woman, and what
more do you want? That plain girl behind, pulling out the drawer, is the eldest
daughter* KATE. *She was disappointed a
few years back on the head of a match
was made up for her and broken afterwards with a farmer from the east of the*

4

county. Some dispute it was about the fortune, and he married a publican's daughter in the latter end. 'Tisn't likely KATE will ever marry, she's up to thirty-six by this time, with a grey streak in her hair and two pushing sisters behind her, but she's a quiet poor thing, no harm in her at all, very useful in the house, I'm told. I'm sure the mother'd be hard set to manage without her.

You're admiring the furniture? 'Twas got five years ago at the Major's auction. A big price they had to pay for it too, GEORGE didn't want to buy it but the mother's heart was set on it. They got new horse-hair put on the arm chair, the Major had it wore to the wood sitting all day over the fire, cursing the Government and drinking whiskey; the six plain chairs are as good as new.

Aren't the pictures lovely? They're all enlarged photographs of WILLIAM'S family. That's WILLIAM himself over the chimney-piece, and that's his brother that died in Boston hanging between the window and the door. The priest in the plush frame is FATHER MAGUIRE, no relation but a lovely man. There's one fancy picture, there on our right, "The Siesta" it's called—two young women asleep in some sort of a fancy dress.

5

WILLIAM *bought the piano when he got married, I'm told it was old* DOCTOR PURCELL'S. *Anyway it's a real old piano; the youngest girl, Baby, is a great one for music. The table's mahogany, the same as the chairs, only you can't see it by reason of the cloth. They're after setting the tea; they got that lamp new this afternoon, isn't it giving great light? Begob, there's a chicken and a shape and apples and a cake—it must be the way they're expecting company.*

Oh, the old one? That's HANNAH. *There's not a house in the village she hasn't been servant in. She was at a hotel in Cork once. Two days they kept her.*]

HANNAH.

Will I bring in the ham, ma'am?

MRS. GEOG.

Do. Reach me down the silver teapot, Kate.

[*'Tisn't real silver, of course, only one of them white metal ones, but catch* MRS. GEOGHEGAN *calling it anything but the purest silver. She's smelling it.*]

There's a sort of musty smell from it.

6

KATE

Sure we haven't used it since Denis was here in the summer?

MRS. GEOG.

I'll make Hannah scald it. . . . God help us, is that the kitchen clock striking six?

KATE

Ah, that clock is always apt to be a bit fast. Anyway the train isn't due till the quarter, and it being market-day, 'twill be a queer thing if it's not ten minutes late, or more.

[HANNAH'S *in again with the ham.*]

MRS. GEOG.

Put it there. Now run across to Mrs. O'Connell's, like a good girl, and ask her to oblige me with a couple of fresh eggs. Tell her it's for Denis they are, and she'll not refuse you.

HANNAH.

There was a duck egg left over from the dinner.

MRS. GEOG.

A duck egg! Isn't it well you know Denis

7

has no stomach at all for coarse food? Be off across the street this minute.

HANNAH.

I will, ma'am.

MRS. GEOG.

Here, carry the teapot before you, and give it a good scalding; 'tis half musty.

HANNAH.

I will ma'am. (*And off with her*)

MRS. GEOG.

Where's Baby?

KATE.

She's above in the room, writing.

MRS. GEOG.

Musha! writing and writing. Isn't it a wonder she wouldn't come down and be readying the place before her brother?

KATE.

Ah, what harm? 'Twon't take us two minutes to finish this.

8

[*This tall girl coming in is* JANE. *She has a year or two less than* KATE. *A nice, quiet girl. She and* DONOUGH BROSNAN *have been promised to each other these years past. Is it chrysanthemums she has in her hand?*]

JANE.

These are all Peg Turpin had. She stripped two plants to get them.

MRS. GEOG.

They're not much indeed, but Denis always had a liking for flowers. Put them there in the middle of the table.

JANE.

That's what Peg was saying. She remembered the way when he was a little child he'd come begging to her for a flower for his coat, and never could she refuse him.

MRS. GEOG.

Refuse him! And why would she refuse him? . . . Bring me the toasting-fork, Kate. I'll make the bit of toast here; 'twill be hotter.

[*Kate's off to the kitchen now. Amn't I after telling you she's a great help to her mother?*]

9

JANE.

I met Aunt Ellen up the street.

MRS. GEOG.

For goodness' sake! Did she say she was coming here?

JANE.

She did.

MRS. GEOG.

Oh, then, bad luck to her, what a night she'd choose to come here! Where are we to put her to sleep?

JANE.

If we put Denis to sleep in the room with George and Peter——

MRS. GEOG.

You'll do no such thing. I'll not have Denis turned out of his room. The three of you girls must sleep together in the big bed; that's the only way we can manage. . . . What crazy old scheme has Ellen in her head this time, I wonder?

JANE.

She didn't tell me, but by her manner I know she's up to something.

10

Mrs. Geog.

God help us! And Denis will be making game of her, and maybe she won't leave him the bit of money after all . . . There's a man's voice—'tis Denis.

[*What a hurry she's in to open the door.*]

Ah, it's only Donough.

[*He's not much to look at, is he? A simple poor fellow, it's a wonder he had the spunk to think of getting married at all.* JANE *could have done better for herself, but she thinks the world of the little man. God knows what she sees in him. Aren't women queer, the fancies they take?*]

Donough.

Good-night, to you.

[*Here's* KATE *back with the toasting-fork.*]

Jane.

Good-night, Donough.

Donough.

Good-night, Jane. Have you your tea taken?

Jane.

I haven't.

Donough.

I wanted you to come across to the Temperance Hall to the concert. I didn't think I could get off in time, but I can. Swallow your tea and come on.

Jane.

Oh, Donough, I'd like to, but, you see, Denis is coming on the six o'clock.

Donough.

Yerra, Denis will keep. Get your hat and come on.

Mrs. Geog.

What's that, Donough? Jane, where are you going?

Jane.

Nowhere, mother. Donough wanted me to go to the concert with him.

Mrs. Geog.

She couldn't go out to-night, thank you, Donough. She must be here to look after Denis.

Jane.

I'd better stay, Donough.

MRS. GEOG.

To-morrow night, now, she'd be delighted.
And maybe Denis would go with the two of
you. That would be nice, now.

DONOUGH.

Oh, faith, that would be grand—grand entirely! Only, you see, there's no concert to-
morrow night.

MRS. GEOG.

Isn't that a pity, and Denis so fond of music.
. . . . I left a drop of cream on the kitchen
table; fetch it for me, Kate.

JANE.

Stay and have a cup of tea, Donough.

MRS. GEOG.

Sure, I suppose the man had his tea an hour
ago.

DONOUGH.

I had, indeed, Mrs. Geoghegan. I'll say
good-night to you. Take care of Denis.
(*He is going.*)

JANE.

I'll see you as far the door, Donough.

[*They're gone.*]

13

MRS. GEOG.

What at all was Jane thinking of, asking a stranger to stop to tea to-night?

KATE.

What stranger? Is it Donough? Sure he's like one of the family, and will be in real earnest the day he marries Jane.

MRS. GEOG.

I'm wondering sometimes what sort of a husband will he make her.

KATE.

The best in the world.

MRS. GEOG.

I don't know. He's a queer, selfish man. Wanting Jane to go out with him to-night. (*She's going to the door.*) Hannah! Hannah! . . . God help us, she'll be all night gossiping at O'Connell's. (*She's listening at the door.*) Who's that going out?

A VOICE.

It's me, mother.

14

MRS. GEOG.

Come in here to me, Baby.

[*Here she comes. Isn't she a great
lump of a girl? She's thirty if she's a
day, but she doesn't look it—'tis the way
she dresses I suppose. She's a great idea
of herself entirely, it's as much as the
mother can do to hold her in. A long envelope she has in her hand.*]

BABY.

Can I do anything for you?

MRS. GEOG.

We're through now, Baby, small thanks to
you. Where are you off to?

BABY.

Only to Duffy's to post this.

MRS. GEOG.

Is it love-letters you were writing all day?

BABY.

You know well it wasn't. Only my shorthand for Skerry's.

15

MRS. GEOG.

Shorthand, moyah! I'd sooner they were love-letters. I've heard it said Thomas Naughton married Julia Roche for her lucky hand with butter, but I never heard yet of a man marrying a girl for shorthand.

BABY.

I'm not wishing to get married, thank you. It's not my intention to spend my days in Bal-lycolman. Up to Dublin I'm going, and if I marry there, it's a gentleman I'll marry—a gentleman who works in an office. (*That's Baby for you!*)

MRS. GEOG.

Tell Jane to come in out of that. She's at the door saying good-night to Donough for the last half hour. (*Off she goes.*)

MRS. GEOG.

Kate, what did I ever do to have such a fool for a daughter?

KATE.

Ah, she's young; little more than a child.

MRS. GEOG.

Faith, it's time she learned sense. . . .

16

Now, if Hannah would bring the eggs we'd be ready. You brought in the drop of cream?

KATE.

It was here all along, mother.

> [*Here's* ELLEN GEOGHEGAN *herself along with* JANE. *You could tell from her appearance the sort she is, a bit cranky and a nasty twist to her tongue if she liked, full of notions and schemes, she's a terrible one for reading; 'tis that has her head turned, there's not a week she hasn't the "Free Press," the "Eagle," and the Supplement to the "Examiner" read to the bone. Still and all, she's a woman to be respected, she must have a couple of hundred acres back there at Kilmurray, and 'tis she owns them three small houses at the other end of the village. . . . Yes, indeed, a wonder she never married—too many notions, may be.*]

JANE.

Here's Aunt Ellen.

MRS. GEOG.

How are you, Ellen? I hope you're good?

> [*How sweet they are, kissing!*]

AUNT ELLEN.

I'm grand, thank you. How are all of you. Will it bother you to put me up for the night?

MRS. GEOG.

Not the least bit in the world.

AUNT ELLEN.

I've a lot to talk over with you all.

MRS. GEOG.

You have? And you'll see Denis. We're expecting him from Dublin any minute.

AUNT ELLEN.

Is that a fact? Did he pass his examination?

MRS. GEOG.

He did. At least, he told me he'd be sure to pass.

AUNT ELLEN.

That's good news. Twice he's failed.

MRS. GEOG.

Small blame to him if he did. He got a sort of a weakness the first time—too hard he was working, Ellen—and the last time there was a cross old fellow examining. Denis told me he

18

couldn't come round him at all; nothing he said would please him. Isn't it a wonder, Ellen, they'd have such a cross man to examine them?

Aunt Ellen.

I'm told Dublin doctors are a fright for crossness. Sure, there was a First Aid class over at my own place, and a doctor from Dublin came down to examine them. Well, three girls was all he would pass out of the twenty, and one of them had a brother a medical and a mother who went mad and drowned herself, so she was experienced like. But as to the lads, divil a one would wait to be examined after they heard how the girls had fared; they took to their heels and up to the mountains with them. Oh, Dublin doctors!

Mrs. Geog.

I tell you then, they're clever men. No one knows that better than myself after all I went through the time Denis was born. And it's up in Dublin Denis will be when he's a doctor. He'll never be one of your common dispensaries, hat in hand to every guardian in the country.

Aunt Ellen.

You're right, Ann, you're right. He's a
19

sight too clever for that. . . . But, tell me, are George and Peter inside?

Mrs. Geog.

George didn't come up from the shop yet, and Peter went down to the station to meet Denis. George will be up for his tea any minute.

Aunt Ellen.

I want to speak to them. I've a great plan in my head. (*Look at them all looking at each other. She has them wore out with her plans.*)

Mrs. Geog.

Don't tell me, Ellen, that 'tis goats again. I was thinking the other day it was only by the help of God you got shut of those queer outlandish goats you had.

Aunt Ellen.

I haven't had a goat these two years.

Mrs. Geog.

'Tis well for you.

Kate.

Another time you were for making a fortune out of tobacco.

20

JANE.

Another time it was Muscovy ducks—cross, wild things; they had me in dread every time I went to see you.

AUNT ELLEN.

Well, I have spirit in me and independence. I'm not like the common farmer people, plodding on in the same old rut from generation to generation.

MRS. GEOG.

Don't mind the children, Ellen. It's only joking they are. Tell us what's on your mind now.

AUNT ELLEN.

Well, I've been reading a deal lately about co-operation.

MRS. GEOG.

What?

AUNT ELLEN.

Co-operation. They say it will be the salvation of Ireland.

MRS. GEOG.

Wisha, don't believe them. They're always blowing about this, that, and the other, and

saying it's to be the salvation of the country.
Sure, they must be talking, the creatures. In
my young days it was the Land League; then
it was Parnell; a couple of years ago 'twas
them Sinn Feiners were to save us, or John
Redmond—I don't rightly remember which. I
wouldn't believe one of them. Pull away and
do your work and put money in the Bank;
that's the only thing to do. Anyway, George
says co-operation will be the ruin of us.
(*She's a rock of sense, that woman.*)

Aunt Ellen.

Well, I'm surprised at him, and he a shop-
keeper and a farmer. By all accounts, it
should be a great lift to him. Anyway, my
co-operatoin is going to be a lift to the family.
Listen here to me, Ann . . .

> [*Here's* George *now. The eldest of
> the family. A steady man, a bit soured,
> maybe, but who wouldn't be and that
> string of sisters depending on him. He
> was forty last summer, but he looks
> more.*]

George.

Is the tea ready, mother?

Mrs. Geog.

We'll have it the very minute Denis comes.

GEORGE.

I didn't see you, Aunt Ellen.   How are you.

AUNT ELLEN.

I'm good, thanks.   You're looking well.

GEORGE.

I can't wait, mother.   Let me have a cup of tea.   I have to go back to the shop.

MRS. GEOG.

Don't sit there, like a good boy; you'll toss the table.   (*But he sits all the same.*)

GEORGE.

Ham, chicken, apples, a cake—is it a party?

MRS. GEOG.

Not at all—only Denis coming, and he'll want a bit after the journey.

AUNT ELLEN.

You spoil Denis, Ann.   He was always your whiteheaded boy.

MRS. GEOG.

Indeed he's nothing of the kind.   I don't make a pin's point of difference between one

23

child and another. . . . Hannah would give
you a nice cup of tea in the kitchen, George.
There's bread-and-butter there, and a lovely
duck egg was left over from the dinner. Run
and tell her, Kate.

GEORGE.

I'll go myself.

AUNT ELLEN.

Stay here a minute. I've been telling your
mother of a great plan I have.

[*There's* KATE *off to give the message.
Didn't I tell you that's the sort she was?*]

GEORGE.

What ails you now.

AUNT ELLEN.

Did you ever hear of a co-operative shop,
George?

GEORGE.

I did. I'd have nothing to do with one of
them.

AUNT ELLEN.

Why?

24

GEORGE.

They're bad. Ruining honest traders, that's what they're doing.

AUNT ELLEN.

Is that a fact? Well, we're starting one over at Kilmurray.

GEORGE.

You are?

AUNT ELLEN.

Up there in the mountains you know how hard it is for us to get anything. Sylvester Brannigan is the only one who's by way of being a trader, and God knows I wouldn't have it on my conscience that I called him an honest one. So a lot of us have joined together and we're going to open a store there. It's going to be a great thing for the family.

GEORGE.

How so?

AUNT ELLEN.

The papers say that half the success of a co-operative shop depends on the manager. We're going to give a good salary to our manager—up to £150 a year—and there's a small house and an acre of land.

GEORGE.

And who is he to be?

AUNT ELLEN.

Your own brother, Peter.

GEORGE.

Peter!

MRS. GEOG.

For goodness' sake!

AUNT ELLEN

Isn't he just the man for the place? He knows all about a shop; he's clever and hard-working, and if he was out of this, Donough could marry Jane and come in and work in his place.

JANE.

Oh, Aunt Ellen, aren't you the great woman for plans!

AUNT ELLEN.

A minute ago I was the greatest old fool in the world.

MRS. GEOG.

I hear steps in the street. Run out, Jane, and see if it's the train after coming in.

[JANE'S *off*.]

26

Would it cost a deal of money, Ellen, to get that place? I suppose there'd be an amount of canvassing to be done?

AUNT ELLEN.

Not at all. Isn't Jamesy Walshe, Donough's mother's cousin? Won't he want Peter to get it? Isn't Patrick Hogan married to John Duffy's sister, and is he likely to be unfriendly to Denis's brother, to the brother of the man his niece, Delia Duffy, is going to marry? Not at all. And then there's myself, who started the whole thing. I tell you, Peter wouldn't be called on to spend as much as half-a-crown in a public-house.

GEORGE.

It might suit Peter all right.

MRS. GEOG.

But, George, if them co-operative things are as bad as you say, maybe we oughtn't to let Peter be mixed up in them.

GEORGE.

Sure, somebody's got to get that £150, and we might as well get it as another. God knows we want money badly. I'm striving to put enough by for Jane's marriage—and now

27

nothing will do Baby but to hyse up to Dublin learning book-keeping or shorthand or something.

AUNT ELLEN.

Glory be to God! Is it notions she has?

GEORGE.

Ay, notions. But they're notions that cost me money, and it costs a lot to make Denis a doctor.

AUNT ELLEN.

Well, the Creegans made their son a doctor, and I'm sure they're in a very small way.

MRS. GEOG.

Is it that little snipeen of a fellow—Joe Creegan? Sure you wouldn't put him alongside my Denis. He's no smartness.

GEORGE.

Denis is smart enough to run up debits in Dublin·

AUNT ELLEN.

Debts!

GEORGE.

Ay, and betting on horses.

28

Mrs. Geog.

From the time he was a little fellow he was always fond of horses, Ellen. I remember well one day, and he little more than a baby——

George.

Well, he's a bit too damned fond of them for me.

[*Here's* Kate *back.*]

Kate.

I've a nice cup of tea for you ready in the kitchen

George.

Thank you, Kate. We'll speak again about this, Aunt. You're staying the night, I suppose?

Aunt Ellen.

I am.

[*And* Baby *and* Jane *in now.*]

Baby.

How are you, Aunt Ellen. (*More kissing.*) Mr. Duffy gave me this at the Post Office. I suppose it's for you, George. *'Tis a telegram.*)

29

Mrs. Geog.

A telegram! Oh, has something happened to Denis? I knew he should be here before this—— Oh, George, what is it at all at all?

Jane.

Be easy, mother.

[*She's all in a flutter. Wisha, she's cracked about* Denis. *'Tisn't so easy to stir* George. . . . *He's read it now.*]

George.

It's not from Denis, at all. . . . But I think it's for him.

Mrs. Geog.

What's in it?

George.

"Hard luck. Geoghegan's Hope also ran. Sorry. Flanagan."

Mrs. Geog.

What does that mean?

George.

I know no more than yourself.

30

Aunt Ellen.

Show me it.   There doesn't seem sense or meaning in it.

Jane.

You've some idea in your head about it, George?

George.

I have.   It's my belief it's about a horse-race.   It's my belief Denis has been betting again.   (*He'll be losing his temper in a minute.*)

Kate.

He wouldn't.   He gave you his word he wouldn't.

Aunt Ellen.

'Tis a terrible curse.   I read on "The Eagle" only last week of a young man who shot himself on the head of all the money he lost on horses.

Mrs. Geog.

You frighten me, Ellen.

George.

You need have no fear of Denis.   He'll not be the one to pay; 'tis us will have to do that.

31

BABY.

That's a fact.

GEORGE.

It'll be the last time. I'm damned if——

KATE.

Hush, hush, George!

[JANE'S *looking at the telegram now.*]

JANE.

Flanagan. That's the name of the young gentleman came to see Denis on a motor bicycle last summer.

MRS. GEOG.

I remember him myself. A lovely young gentleman. Seemingly he had a great liking for Denis—he talked to me about him for a long time, half laughing like. The "hope of the Geoghegans" he called him.

GEORGE.

What's that? The "hope of the Geoghegans"? Did he call him that?

32

MRS. GEOG.

He did. Denis told me 'twas a sort of a pet name he put on him in college.

JANE.

What is it, George?

GEORGE.

"Geoghegan's Hope also ran." That's either a race horse, or it's Denis himself.

JANE.

I don't understand you.

GEORGE.

He's either broken his word to me and is betting on horses, or else . . . he's failed again.

JANE.

His examination, you mean?

GEORGE.

I do.

JANE.

God help us!

MRS. GEOG.

Yerra, he hasn't failed. Don't think it,

George. He told me himself last week in a letter he'd be certain to pass.

KATE.

'Twould be terrible for him if he failed.

BABY.

'Twould be terrible for us, you mean.

MRS. GEOG.

He'd never break his word to you about the betting.

GEORGE.

For his own sake I'd almost hope he had. For if this isn't about a horse, if it's about Denis himself, if it means he's failed, I'll—I'll——

MRS. GEOG.

You're speaking very cross, George, about your brother.

GEORGE.

I have reason to speak cross. If he's failed for the third time, divil another penny will he get from me—except his passage to Canada.

> [*They're staring at him; they don't believe him.*]

34

I mean it. You're all looking at me as if I was out of my senses. It's out of our senses we've been all these years and years, spending lashings of money on an idle, good-for-nothing young fellow.

MRS. GEOG.

Yerra, George! . . .

GEORGE.

From the day he was born, hasn't everything been given to him? Look at the whips of money laid by for his education. He was too grand and too clever to be sent to the National School like the rest of us—poor Mr. Lacy didn't know enough to teach him; oh, no! he had to go into the city every day by train—second-class—to be taught by the Christian Brothers. Look at Kate there, worn and grey before her time, an old maid. Wouldn't she have been married ten years ago to Jer Connor only we hadn't a penny to give with her, it all being kept for the laddo, to send him to college, Trinity College, nothing less would be fitting of course. And what's there to show for it all? Nothing at all. He doesn't even pass his examinations. What's keeping Jane from marrying Donough, only Denis? What's keeping Baby at home, and she mad to be learning up in Dublin, only Denis? What's

35

keeping us straitened and pinching and saving, only Denis, Denis, Denis? But the old horse learns its lesson in the end, and I've learnt mine. Not another red halfpenny will he get from me. You can tell him that when he comes in.

> [*And off with him, banging the door after him.*]

Mrs. Geog.

Ellen, what's come to him at all to speak like that?

Baby.

It's true what he says. Every word of it's true.

Mrs. Geog.

Hold your tongue, girl!

> [*That's one for* Baby, *she's flouncing out of the room.*]

Kate, run after your brother and pacify him.

> [*She's gone, but what can she do, the creature?*]

What's come to him at all at all?

Aunt Ellen.

'Tis true, you always made a pet of the boy —but sure we all did. I was reading in the

36

"Girl's Friend" not long ago how foolish it was for a mother to be making differences between her children. They said that—

Mrs. Geog.

And why shouldn't I make differences? Is there anyone living who'd stand up on the floor and say that Denis isn't smarter and cleverer than his two brothers—or his sisters, either—or the whole menagerie of the Geoghegans lumped together? From the day he was born I knew he was different. Oh, Ellen, it will break my heart if George turns against him now! (*Is it crying she is?*)

Aunt Ellen.

Quiet yourself, Ann. . . . Go out, Jane, and speak to your brother. He always had respect for you.

Jane.

I'll see what mood he is in. (*She's gone after him—she knows how to humour him.*)

Mrs. Geog.

From the day he was born I knew he was different. I was getting an old woman when he came . . . you remember, Ellen; it was nearly ten years after Baby was born. I

37

thought I'd never have another child; it seemed like a miracle. . . . I thought I'd die with it.

AUNT ELLEN.

You were nervous, I remember that.

MRS. GEOG.

Nervous? I was mad afraid. My sister—poor Bridgie—made me go up to Dublin to see a doctor there. Oh, Ellen, that doctor was a lovely man. He was a sort of a lord, Sir Denis Bellingham Burke, that was his name. He'd have nothing to do with common cases, 'twould be no use going to him with a broken leg or a sick stomach or the like—he wouldn't look at you. Women like me, those are all he'd see, and he told me . . .

[*She's whispering. We oughtn't to listen: 'Tis no place for us.*]

AUNT ELLEN.

I remember your telling me that at the time. It was surprising.

MRS. GEOG.

Wasn't it now? Well, I did every mortal thing he told me to. I went into a sort of hospital—I'd be afraid to tell you what they made me pay—but I had the best of everything, and when Denis was born I called him after the dear doctor.

AUNT ELLEN.

And made up your mind to make a doctor of him.

MRS. GEOG.

I did. 'Twas like a miracle, a boy to come after all those three lumps of girls. . . . He was a lovely child . . . and now if George turns against him! Sure he has the money, and can do what he likes. Denis away in Canada! 'Twould break my heart.

[KATE's *back.*]

KATE.

He's ramping and raging in the kitchen. He says if the telegram is true, if he's missed his examination, he'll ship him off next week.

MRS. GEOG.

I'll go to George myself. I'll talk him over. He can't be in earnest. And what about Delia Duffy? Isn't he promised to her as soon as ever he's a doctor? Is she to be shipped to Canada along with him? Where's George? I'll go to him.

[*God help* GEORGE *when he meets her.*

Ah! here's DENIS *in the other door. Isn't he lovely? You'd know he was from Dublin by his clothes and his smartness. He's just turned twenty-two.*]

DENIS.

Hullo, mother!

MRS. GEOG.

Denis my darling boy! (*She's flinging her arms round his neck; she'll have him choked.*)

DENIS.

Hold on, mother—or, rather, don't hold on! Don't kill me altogether!

MRS. GEOG.

How are you, my poor boy?

DENIS.

Top hole. Hullo Aunt Ellen; this is an unexpected pleasure. (*I'd say he was codding her from the way he kissed her.*) Well, Kate.

[*This young girl coming in is* DELIA DUFFY. *She's not as simple as she looks. She's her father's daughter. The fellow with her carrying all the luggage is* PETER

GEOGHEGAN, *he's nothing much one way or the other.*]

PETER.

Where will I leave these?

DENIS.

Oh, chuck them up into my room, like a good chap. Here I'll give you this coat.

[*Poor* PETER.]

MRS. GEOG.

Oh, Delia, I didn't see you. Come in and sit down. You went to the station, I suppose?

DELIA.

I did. I can't wait, Mrs. Geoghegan, thanks.

MRS. GEOG.

Yerra, stay and have a cup of tea.

DELIA.

I must be off home to give my father his supper. Denis will come down and see me later. There's questions I want to ask him. I have it in my mind he's been carrying on with a young lady in Dublin. (*She is going.*)

41

DENIS.

Delia, I swear . . .

DELIA.

Ssh! Don't tell lies on an empty stomach; wait till after tea.

[*She's gone.*]

DENIS.

But, Delia, I . . .

[*He's gone after her, she has him in good order.*]

AUNT ELLEN.

He's looking gay enough now. Little he knows what's before him!

MRS. GEOG.

Oh, Ellen!

[*Here's* GEORGE, JANE, *and* BABY.]

JANE.

Has he come?

AUNT ELLEN.

He has.

42

MRS. GEOG.

George, you won't be hard on him? He's dead tired and hungry.

GEORGE.

Did he say anything about the examination?

MRS. GEOG.

He didn't; it's likely he doesn't know. It'll break his heart when he finds out he's failed— if failed he has. Couldn't we keep it from him for a day or two?

JANE.

It's better he should know it, mother. George is right. It's time a change was made.

MRS. GEOG.

Jane!

JANE.

You never think, maybe, I'd want my chance as well as Denis. You never think, maybe, Donough will get tired waiting.

[*You wouldn't think* JANE *could be so bitter.*]

BABY.

And I'm not going to stay in this hole of a place any longer.

43

MRS. GEOG.

You're an unnatural family, that's what you are!

[DENIS *is back; he has a box of cigars in his hand.*]

DENIS.

What's the confabulation about? Have you a match, George?

MRS. GEOGH.

Tell Hannah to bring in the tea.

[*Of course it's* KATE *that goes.*]

DENIS.

Beastly cold, isn't it?

[*Look at them moving aside so that he can have the centre of the fire.*]

Well, Aunt Ellen, what's the latest? Is it true you've been making a fortune turning turf into paper?

AUNT ELLEN.

It isn't

DENIS.

I'm surprised to hear that. A wide-awake woman like you, with a bog of your own.

44

You should keep moving, Aunt Ellen, keep moving

AUNT ELLEN.

Thank you for your advice.

GEORGE.

Aunt Ellen has some regard for the family. She's got a good position in her eye for Peter.

DENIS.

What's that?

AUNT ELLEN.

Manager of a shop, a co-operative shop.

DENIS.

Co-operation? I see. That's the latest Sir What's-his-name, the hairy poet chap and all the rest of the gang—they'll suit you down to the ground, Aunt Ellen. They're just your sort.

AUNT ELLEN.

Do you know them?

DENIS.

Me? No—thank God!

45

GEORGE.

It's time some of us made a little money.

DENIS.

Oh, if there's money in it. I'm sure there's no one knows better than I do how much we want money.

MRS. GEOG.

Poor boy!

GEORGE.

No one knows better than you do how to spend it.

DENIS.

Well, it's made to be spent, isn't it? What are you grousing about, anyway? Look what I brought you. (*He's giving him the box of cigars.*) They're good ones, too.

MRS. GEOG.

Oh, George, isn't it good of Denis? He never forgets you. (*She's glad of the chance to soften* GEORGE.)

DENIS.

Wait till you see what I have upstairs in my bag for you, mother.

46

GEORGE.

Thank you, but I'd rather you wouldn't spend your money—I mean my money—on me.

DENIS.

Oh, I've been jolly economical lately. I don't believe I've had more than ten pounds from you since the summer.

GEORGE.

Ten! You believe queer things.

DENIS.

Well, not more than twenty—or twenty-five.

GEORGE.

Tell me this: have you been betting lately?

MRS. GEOG.

George!

DENIS.

No. Honour bright. Never once since you gave me that rowing. Though I don't mind telling you I missed a good thing last week; could have made twenty pounds as easily as lighting a cigarette.

47

JANE.

You're sure you weren't betting?

DENIS.

Absolutely. . . . Why you all look disappointed . . . as if you wished I had been . . . What's the matter?

GEORGE.

What does this mean so? (*He's giving him the telegram.*)

DENIS.

A wire? Is it for me?

GEORGE.

Read it and see.

DENIS.

Oh, I suppose it's from Flanagan. He said he'd wire the result of the exam.; it wasn't out when I left Dublin.

MRS. GEOG.

Don't mind it, Denis. Have your tea first —'tis nothing at all.

BABY.

Be quiet, mother. Can't you let him read it?

48

GEORGE.

Well?

DENIS.

Oh, I've lost my exam. Isn't that a beastly nuisance? I'm not surprised; I guessed I hadn't got it. (*Faith, it doesn't seem to trouble him.*)

MRS. GEOG.

Never mind, my poor boy. It doesn't matter the least bit in the world.

[HANNAH, KATE *and* PETER *are back.*]

Here's Hannah with the tea. . . . Put this out of your head and have a bit of chicken and a sup of tea.

[*She's coaxing him to the table.*]

Sure, what are those examinations after all? Only cross questions and botheration. I never could see the use of them. Run off and boil an egg, Hannah.

[HANNAH'S *gone.*]

There's a nice hot cup, now. Drink it and don't worry your head over this.

⁴ 49

DENIS.

Oh, I'm not worrying, mother. I'll get it next time to a dead cert. (*He's eating his tea as if nothing had happened.*)

GEORGE.

You won't.

DENIS.

Oh, yes, I will. You'll see. I'll work like a nigger from now till June. Don't worry about it, old chap. Push me over the butter.

GEORGE.

I've done worrying. I've gone through a deal of that in the last few years.

DENIS.

That's right. Take life easy. That's what I do.

GEORGE.

I've been thinking that. It's time you worried round a bit now.

DENIS.

I'll worry till I get this exam. anyway.

GEORGE.

I'm not going to ask you to.

50

THE WHITEHEADED BOY

DENIS.

What do you mean? You're all looking
dashed solemn. What is it?

[*He's beginning to feel there's something up.*]

MRS. GEOG.

Don't mind George, Denis. He's a bit put
out to-night, but——

GEORGE.

Mother! We've been thinking things over;
we think you've been long enough at College;
it's time you left.

DENIS.

Left! Leave Trinity! But I'm only half
through.

GEORGE.

That's not my fault, is it?

DENIS.

But I can't become a doctor. I'm not
qualified.

GEORGE.

I'm not asking you to be a doctor.

51

DENIS.

But . . . what . . . I don't understand.

GEORGE.

Well, here it is in two words. There's been enough and too much money spent on you; I'll spend no more. Yes, I will though—twenty pounds more. That'll pay your passage to Canada and leave a bit in your pocket.

[*That's a slap in the face for him. There's not a word out of him.*]

DENIS.

You're joking.

GEORGE.

I am not.

DENIS.

But . . . but . . . why?

GEORGE.

Because there's a couple of others here to consider as well as yourself. It's fair they should get their chance. You've had yours.

DENIS.

And what am I to do in Canada?

52

GEORGE.

You can find out when you get there. You've a pair of hands, haven't you? When you've an empty belly and a pair of hands, I tell you you won't be long finding something to do.

DENIS.

I see . . . Are you all agreed on this—or is it only George?

MRS. GEOG.

Denis, darling, I'll never desert you.

DENIS.

Are you all agreed on this?

JANE.

I'd be sorry you'd go, but Donough is getting tired waiting for me.

BABY.

You're not the only one wants education. I'm not going to stick in Ballycolman all my life.

KATE.

George is right.

53

AUNT ELLEN.

You've had your chance, Denis, and you've
thrown it away. It's time you turned round
and worked for yourself. Let this be a lesson
to you——

PETER.

It's time I got a look in.

DENIS.

Well, I think it's a damned shame.

[*He'll be losing his temper in a minute.*]

GEORGE.

It's your own fault. You brought it on
yourself.

DENIS.

I didn't. I didn't! I never asked to be sent
to College; I never asked to have all this money
spent on me. I'd have been content to live here
with the rest of you——

PETER.

You were too clever for the like of us.

MRS. GEOG.

Different altogether.

54

Denis.

I wasn't.

Aunt Ellen.

To look at you standing there amongst them, Denis, 'tis easy seen how different you are

Denis.

Yes, I'm different now, but whose fault is that? It's not mine. Who was it made me out to be so clever; who insisted on making a doctor of me, or sending me to Trinity? It was all of you. From the time I was a baby you treated me as if I was something wonderful, and now when you find I'm not what you thought I was you kick me out—across the sea to Canada, where you'll never hear of me again. You give me the education of a gentleman, lashings of money in my pocket, no wish denied me, and in the end you tell me I'm to be a labourer.

George.

There's other work besides farming in Canada.

Denis.

It's unfair.

Mrs. Geog.

I won't let you go, Denis.

DENIS.

Oh, I'll go fast enough, never fear. We all know what George is when he's made up his mind about a thing. He made up his mind I was to go to College to be a doctor, and I went. Now he's made up his mind I'm to go to Canada, and I'll go. He's got the purse; he can do what he likes.

AUNT ELLEN.

If you weren't a fool you wouldn't be saying these things; he might do great things for you yet if he had a mind to.

DENIS.

I'm asking no favours from him. I'll not take a shilling from him. I'll get enough some other way to take me out of this; don't be afraid you'll be bothered with me. I'll go back to Dublin to-morrow.

MRS. GEOG.

Denis!

DENIS.

I'll be free, anyway, from this to make my own life in my own way. I'm tired of other people managing it for me.

56

GEORGE.

You're vexed with me now. Some day you'll be very thankful to me.

DENIS.

I've no doubt I will. You're giving me a great opening. I'm tremendously obliged to you all.

MRS. GEOG.

It breaks my heart to hear you talk so bitter. And Delia—what'll Delia say at all to all this?

DENIS.

Delia? Oh, you may be sure George has some plan in his head for Delia. She's to go to South Africa, I suppose, or maybe he's arranged to marry her himself.

GEORGE.

I've no wish to part you. She can marry you and go to Canada if she's willing. I'll pay the passage for the two of you.

DENIS.

Thank you for nothing. I'm asking no money from you, and I've no intention of asking Delia to come out and rough it in Canada. She wasn't brought up to that sort of thing.

57

PETER.

John Duffy would give you money with her maybe. Enough to set the two of you up in Canada.

DENIS.

I'm asking no favours from John Duffy or from any of you. I'll tell Delia the truth; tell her I'm being kicked out by my family because I'm good for nothing. I'll make an end of the whole thing. I'll write to Delia to-night, this very minute—I'll go back to Dublin in the morning; I'll not stay another night here.

AUNT ELLEN.

This is hard for you, Denis, but maybe it's the best thing that could happen.

DENIS.

That's it, Aunt Ellen, the best thing in the world for all of us. Peter will go out to you, Donough will marry Jane, Baby will go to Dublin; there'll be plenty of money for everything. Denis will be—well, it doesn't matter a damn where Denis will be. He'll be out of the way, at any rate. Babe, darling, get me a sheet of paper and an envelope.

MRS. GEOG.

My heart's broken between you all.
58

KATE.

Don't take on mother.

[BABY'S *brought him the paper.*]

DENIS.

Thanks, Babe; you're a jewel. Look out for yourself when you go to Dublin; all the fellows in Skerry's will be mad after you. There's something really fascinating about you.

[*How bitter he is! Look at the toss of her head. They're watching him writing. AUNT ELLEN'S got the girls round her; she's speaking in a low voice to them.*]

AUNT ELLEN.

I don't think he should write that to Delia about his being turned out. Great laughing the neighbours will be having at us, and all the talk we made of his cleverness for the last twenty years.

KATE.

There's truth in that, Aunt Ellen.

BABY.

I'd be ashamed to be seen on the street for the next twelvemonth, and all we've been blowing about him.

PETER.

There's that little loan I got partly on the good prospects of Mister Denis.

AUNT ELLEN.

If you'll take my advice you'll give out that he's gone out to a good position in Canada. I had a brother there once, twenty-five years ago. He died without a child. No matter. Can't you say Denis has gone out to his cousins—that they're in a big way of business? That will save your face.

[*A great idea, sure enough.*]

JANE.

You're a great woman for schemes, Aunt.

GEORGE.

It's a good idea. We don't want to be disgraced out and out.

BABY.

People to laugh at me—'twould make me mad.

AUNT ELLEN.

Do you hear what we're saying, Denis?

Denis.

I do. It's nothing to me what lie I leave behind me. I don't care if they know the truth
about me. But you can have your own way
in this, too. I've told her I'm off to Canada
in two days, and we can't get married. I'll put
a postscript to say I'm going out to a big
position.

Aunt Ellen.

It's a pity you're so hasty. Delia is a good
match; you shouldn't throw her away so smart.

[*He's got the letter done.*]

Denis.

There! Send Hannah down to Duffy's with
it.

[Jane *goes to the door.*]

Jane.

Hannah, come here a minute.

George.

Before you send it, Denis, think again over
what I've said. I know you're fond of Delia;
I don't want to come between you. Marry her;
I'll send you both to Canada, and I'll put a bit
of money in your hand.

61

DENIS.

You've washed your hands of me, George. You and Delia have got to take the consequences of it as well as I.

[*Here's* HANNAH *with an egg.*]

Take that note down to Duffy's, Hannah.

HANNAH.

I will. There's your egg. 'Tisn't laid two hours, and Mrs. O'Connell says she'll send you in one every day as long as you're here.

DENIS.

I'll be putting no strain on her hens, Hannah. I'm off to-morrow.

HANNAH.

To-morrow! Yerra——

AUNT ELLEN.

To Canada he's going, Hannah. To a grand position there with his uncle's eldest son.

HANNAH.

Canada! For godness' sake! And is he not going doctoring?

62

AUNT ELLEN.

This is better than doctoring. A great position he'll have. You can be off now. Tell everyone you meet about Denis.

HANNAH.

I will, to be sure. I'm delighted, Mister Denis, things have turned out so well for you. Delia Duffy will be burning the house down for pure joy to-night. I'll be off as fast as my legs can carry me. (*God knows that's not saying much. Still when she's got a bit of gossip she'll lose no time.*)

GEORGE.

You're feeling bitter about this, Denis. I'm sorry for you. Will you believe me saying I think it's for the best?

DENIS.

You don't care a damn whether I believe you or not. (*That's enough for* GEORGE. *He's going out.*)

MRS. GEOG.

Your tea's cold. Wait till I get you a hot sup. Will you have a bit of chicken?

63

DENIS.

I couldn't eat anything. I wish you'd all leave me alone. You've got all you wanted from me. I'll be gone for ever in the morning.

MRS. GEOG.

You're beat out. You've a headache, maybe?

DENIS.

I have.

MRS. GEOG.

The tea will do you good. I'll get them to make you a piece of hot toast. Kate or Baby, or one of you, run into the kitchen and make a piece of toast—quick.

BABY.

I think it's time Denis learned to make his own toast.

PETER.

I'm not going to make it for him anyway.

JANE.

I've other things to do.

[*Off with them all.*]

Mrs. Geog.

Don't mind them. I'll make the toast for you. It will all come right.

Denis.

It's so unfair—so unfair; that's what I mind.

Mrs. Geog.

It is, it is. (*She's kneeling by the fire toasting bread.*)

Denis.

It was your fault first, mother. You made me out to be something great.

Mrs. Geog.

And aren't you? Is there a lad anywhere as clever as you? Sure, hasn't everyone the same story of your smartness, and they can't all be mistaken.

Denis.

They are.

Mrs. Geog.

Not at all. You'll get what you want in the end. You'll see.

DENIS.

I want nothing at all now except to be let alone.

MRS. GEOG.

My poor boy. . . . I never feel as if the others were my children the way you are.

DENIS.

And I've been a bad son to you.

MRS. GEOG.

You haven't, you haven't. You've never given me a cross word. You mustn't go across the sea to Canada. What would I do without you, and what would poor Delia do?

DENIS.

Poor Delia!

MRS. GEOG.

Every girl in the place is wild about you. They were mad that you'd never look at one of them only Delia Duffy. I never thought she was half good enough for you; I always hoped you'd marry a lady from the city, for all John Duffy has the Post Office and is Chairman of the District Council. . . . But you'd have got money with her.

66

DENIS.

Well, that's all over now.

MRS. GEOG.

The toast is just done. Hold it a minute
and I'll fetch the cup of tea. You can sit there
and be taking it.

[*Here's* KATE *back. She has a piece of
toast on a plate.*]

KATE.

I made a piece of toast at the fire upstairs.

[*And* JANE *in the other door with another piece of toast.*]

JANE.

Denis, will you—— Oh, have you been
making toast?

[*And* HANNAH'S *head in at the door.*]

HANNAH.

Have you the toasting-fork there, ma'am?
Peter wants to make a piece of toast for Mister
Denis.

67

DENIS.

I want none of your toast.   You can keep your bally toast.

[*But he's taking the piece his mother holds out to him.*]

CURTAIN.

Act II

[The same room again later in the even-ing and George *and* Peter *sitting, talking.]*

PETER.

You think I should take it, then?

GEORGE.

I do.

PETER.

But supposing it fails?

GEORGE.

Aunt Ellen will stick to it for a year or two, and by that time it will have failed or succeed-ed. If it's a success, you're game ball; if it fails you're no worse off than you are now, and there will always be foolish, contrary people starting them co-operative things; that class is as thick as thieves and lavish with their money; once you get well in with them they'll not

69

desert you. Besides, you knowing all about shopkeeping, you'll be able to make things easier for the locals. Do you understand me?

PETER.

I do.

GEORGE.

Them co-operatives have never succeeded yet, but if they ever do—'twould be bad days for us. I'd like to see you there for life, and yet 'twouldn't be well to be too successful.

PETER.

Ah, there'll be some sort of a middle course.

[*With a wink.*]

GEORGE.

That's what's in my mind.

PETER.

And Donough will marry Jane and come in here in my place, and Baby will be up in Dublin, and Denis will be off our hands. Faith, it all fits together as neat as a puzzle.

GEORGE.

And you could be giving an eye to Aunt Ellen's bit of land, and not letting her play

70

puck with it with her contrary schemes, and in the end she'll leave it to you, why wouldn't she? She'll forget Denis when the salt water's between them.

PETER.

He's been a weight on us for years; we're well rid of him. But all the same, I felt sorry for the poor fellow to-night.

GEORGE.

Ah, he'll do first-class in Canada, Sure, all sorts does well out there. I'm only afraid of the mother having the life wore out of me fretting after him.

PETER.

She'll get over that in time.

GEORGE.

Well, she must. I'm not going back on what I said about Denis. Go he must.

[*Here's their aunt.*]

AUNT ELLEN.

George, your mother wants you. She's above in her room.

GEORGE.

Is she after going to bed?

AUNT ELLEN.

She is not; she can't get this business of
Denis out of her mind, the creature.

GEORGE.

There's no use in her talking of it to me.
My mind is made up; we're all determined.
Denis must go.

AUNT ELLEN.

Even so, a word from you might quiet her.
Anyhow, she won't take rest till she sees you.

GEORGE.

I'll go to her so.

[*He's gone. 'Tisn't likely there's anything he can say will quiet her.*]

AUNT ELLEN.

You'd have to pity her. Denis was always
her whiteheaded boy, and this is a blow to her.
Well, we must all go through with it. . . .
Tell me, are you coming out to Kilmurray?

72

Peter.

I'm after talking it over with George; he advises me to go.

Aunt Ellen.

He's right. You'll never regret it. I suppose you know all about co-operation?

Peter.

Divil a bit. But I can keep a shop.

Aunt Ellen.

That's all we want.

Peter.

I'll leave you and the Committee to do the co-operating.

Aunt Ellen.

You'd better come back there with me to-morrow. The sooner you see the Committee the better. Not that there's a fear you won't get it, for I mentioned your name to them and they were agreeable; but it's best to make sure of them; you never know when they wouldn't turn round behind your back and put in an ignorant fellow—a fellow who couldn't weigh a pound of sugar—just because he was a relation of one of them. It's one of the curses of the country, giving positions to relations.

PETER.

I agree with you, Aunt.

AUNT ELLEN.

They're a jobbing, ignorant crowd out at Kilmurray. . . . There's a knock. Who can it be this hour of night?

PETER.

Hannah's snoring this half-hour. I'll see who it is.

[*He's gone and here he is back and* JOHN DUFFY *with him.* JOHN *is one of the solidest men in Ballycolman, Chairman of the District Council, Chairman of the Race Committee, and a member of every Committee and every League in the village. He has three public-houses and a grocery business and the Post Office and a branch of the National Bank once a month, and a trade in old hens and eggs and a terrible turn-over in turkeys at Christmas. . . . Oh, a weighty man. . . . Yes, he buried the wife long ago; he's no child but* DELIA. *He's not looking in too pleasant a humour.*]

AUNT ELLEN.

Oh, good evening, Mr. Duffy; you're welcome. I was wondering who the knock might be .

DUFFY.

'Tis late for visits, but I slipped up to see George for a minute.

AUNT ELLEN.

He's in the mother's room. Will you tell him, Peter?

[PETER'S *gone to tell* GEORGE.]

AUNT ELLEN.

Will you sit down, Mr. Duffy? . . . 'Twon't be long to Christmas now.

DUFFY.

That's true.

AUNT ELLEN.

You're looking well. How's Delia these times?

DUFFY.

She's well enough. She got a great throw-over to-night.

AUNT ELLEN.

Is that a fact?

DUFFY.

Is Denis around?

AUNT ELLEN.

He's not.   He's gone to bed.

DUFFY.

He's going from you, I hear?

AUNT ELLEN.

He is indeed, poor boy.   It's hard parting from him, but since it's for his advantage we wouldn't stand in his way.

[*Wouldn't anyone believe her the way she says it?*]

DUFFY.

To be sure, to be sure.

AUNT ELLEN.

I always said he was too clever to be a doctor.   When you see the ignorant fellows that are turned into doctors, you can't believe, Mr. Duffy, that it takes much wit to cut off a man's leg or to give him a bottle of medicine.

76

DUFFY.

There's something in that.

AUNT ELLEN.

Now in Canada he'll find an opening suitable to his smartness. A brother of my own went out there forty years ago and 'tis wonderful the way he got on.

DUFFY.

Is it to his people Denis is going?

AUNT ELLEN.

It is. He left a troop of sons and daughters after him.

DUFFY.

And where do they live?

AUNT ELLEN.

They?—Oh, they live in Saint Paul.

DUFFY.

I thought that was in the States.

AUNT ELLEN.

There's a place of that name in Canada, too. Do you suppose I wouldn't know my own brother's place?

77

DUFFY.

I beg your pardon, ma'am; indeed I meant no such thing. He's in business, I suppose?

AUNT ELLEN.

You may say he is, then. By all accounts he owns half the town.

DUFFY.

Do you tell me? Denis will have a fine position so.

AUNT ELLEN.

Oh, the best in the world. Nothing to do but superintending like, strolling about with his hands in his pockets making other people work and putting money in the Bank all the time.

DUFFY.

Bedad, that sounds a good life. Tell me, what class of business has your brother?

[*That's a facer!*]

AUNT ELLEN.

A mixed business, Mr. Duffy.

[*Good woman!*]

78

DUFFY.

I see.

[*Here's* PETER *back with* GEORGE.]

GEORGE.

You were wanting me, John?

DUFFY.

I was.

GEORGE.

If it's the fertilizer you're after, I didn't get
it in yet. I have it ordered a fortnight or
more.

DUFFY.

'Tisn't that at all. . . . This is great news
about Denis.

GEORGE.

Ay.

DUFFY.

He's off to Canada?

GEORGE.

He is.

DUFFY.

Hannah was blowing about a fine place he's
going to, and your Aunt was saying the same
thing just now. It's a fact, I suppose?

GEORGE.

That's true.

DUFFY.

Lashings of money and nothing to do.

GEORGE.

I believe so.

DUFFY.

His cousins own the town?

GEORGE.

They do.

DUFFY.

'Tis very sudden.

GEORGE.

That's the way things come, John.   Only this evening it was settled.

AUNT ELLEN.

Of course, Denis being so clever, we always looked for something big to turn up for him.

DUFFY.

Delia's in a state over it.

80

GEORGE.

Ah, she needn't be. Indeed, we were all sorry about that, but it couldn't be helped. They were only children, John, and with Denis going off now there was no use going on with it. Delia's a nice little girl; she's too good for Denis——

PETER.

That's a fact.

AUNT ELLEN.

She'll take up with someone who'll be a deal more suitable.

DUFFY.

They've been promised to one another for two years; as soon as he'd be a doctor they were to be married, and now in the heel of the hunt he gets a big position in Canada, he spreads his sails and away with him, leaving her behind. Faith, it looks to me as if you thought she wasn't good enough for him.

[*Didn't I know he was near his temper.*]

GEORGE.

Indeed, John, you're making a mistake. That's not the way with it at all. It's the other way about.

6　　　81

DUFFY.

That's the way I look at it, anyway, and that's the way the neighbours will look at it.

GEORGE.

Sure, it's not cross about it you are?

DUFFY.

Oh no, not at all. There's nothing in the wide world a man likes better than to have his only child trampled on like dirt, to be left fooled, to be made a mock of by the country-side. Cross? What would make me cross? I never felt in a pleasanter temper than I do this minute.

PETER.

You're talking strange.

DUFFY.

The two of you will hear stranger talk than this before you've finished with the Duffy's.

GEORGE.

What do you mean?

DUFFY.

I mean Denis marries Delia, or else . . .

GEORGE.

He can't marry her.

AUNT ELLEN.

Put that notion out of your mind, Mr. Duffy.

DUFFY.

Then if he won't marry her, I put the matter into the lawyer's hands to-morrow. £1,000 damages.

[*Oh, my God!*]

GEORGE.

John!

AUNT ELLEN.

Mr. Duffy!

PETER.

You're raving!

DUFFY.

Ay, you think yourselves great people, don't you? You've a brother who's a gentleman, who is much too high up to get married to a Duffy. It's good enough for Delia to be thrown aside like an old shoe when the fancy takes you. She's not good enough to be brought to Canada, to the fine place there that . . .

GEORGE.

John, wait. I . . .

DUFFY.

But I'll show you you've mistaken your man.
As long as Delia has a father by her she'll not
be treated that way. I'll show you! The
Duffys aren't people to be trampled on
so easy. I've power to my back—and money—
more money than you have—and, by the same
token, I'll see a lump of yours before I'm done
with you. I'll have the smartest lawyer in Ireland on my side. I got all Denis's letters off
Delia to-night—oh, there's no doubt of my
case. I'll beat you to the wall, I'll bleed you,
I'll teach you the way to treat a decent, honest,
poor girl who never did you a day's harm only
demeaned herself mixing with low, sneaking
people the like of the Geoghegans. Good night
to you.

GEORGE.

Stop, for God's sake, Mr. Duffy. You
don't know what you're talking about.

DUFFY.

Faith, I do, only too well.

84

GEORGE.

'Tisn't true. All that about Canada isn't true.

DUFFY.

Isn't he going there?

GEORGE.

He is, but not to . . .

DUFFY.

That's enough about it.

[*He's going out, but* GEORGE *is holding him back.*]

GEORGE.

Don't go. Look here, I'm telling you the truth now, the same as if you were a magistrate on the bench. He's going to no situation there; he's been kicked out of this because we're tired of paying his bills.

DUFFY.

Do you expect me to believe that?

GEORGE.

You must believe it. Aunt Ellen, tell him that what I'm saying is true.

85

AUNT ELLEN.

It's true, every word of it. I've no cousins in Canada, my brother died unmarried, Denis will have to work like a labourer in Canada.

PETER.

We're turning him out; he's a useless, idle fellow.

AUNT ELLEN.

Delia's well rid of him; a burden he'd be to her.

GEORGE.

She'll get a man twice as good before the year's out.

PETER.

He's a waster.

GEORGE.

No sense at all.

PETER.

A gambler, betting all day on horses.

AUNT ELLEN.

Cards and drink.

86

GEORGE.

He has mother's heart broken

PETER.

'Tis a great escape Delia's having.

GEORGE.

They'd be in the Union before they'd be a year married.

AUNT ELLEN.

He's a disgrace to the family.

DUFFY.

Well, what sort of a fool do you take me to be at all? Haven't I two eyes in my head? Don't I know Denis since the day he was born? Isn't he known to be the cleverest, smartest . . .

GEORGE.

Not at all.

DUFFY.

. . . lad in the countryside. Didn't you tell me yourself the way he swept all before him in the College in Dublin?

GEORGE.

'Tisn't true. Three times he's after failing.

DUFFY.

Wasn't he going to be set up there in a big house?

PETER.

Not at all.

DUFFY.

Wasn't his aunt going to leave him all her money?

AUNT ELLEN.

He'll never get a penny from me.

DUFFY.

And now you'd like me to turn around and disbelieve it all. Ah, you're clever, but you're not clever enough for me.

GEORGE.

You're making a mistake. To-night things turned up.

DUFFY.

They did; I know well they did. Canada turned up, a big position turned up, plans and schemes you made to throw us over. I see your game. Tell me George, is Saint Paul the name of the place Denis is going to?

GEORGE.

No.

[*Look at* DUFFY *turning on the aunt.*]

DUFFY.

Didn't I know you were lying, ye old brazen thing the way I wouldn't be able to trace him to bring him back to marry my daughter. But I don't care a damn where he is going to. You're right, Delia's well quit of him; she's well quit of the whole troop of the Geoghegans —but I want that £1,000 and I'll have it too.

PETER.

It's the truth we're telling you, Mr. Duffy. The rest was all lies.

DUFFY.

I know well it's liars you all are.

[*Here's* DONOUGH; *he's excited like.*]

DONOUGH.

I couldn't go home till I'd congratulated you about Denis. All the people at the concert were talking of it. It's over railways he'll be, I'm told; a sort of a railway king.

GEORGE.

Oh, my God!

89

DUFFY.

Do you hear that?

DONOUGH.

George, my mind's made up; I'm going with him. When he has all that power he'll be able to do something for the man that's going to marry his sister. I'm tired of slaving on here and no nearer marrying Jane than I was five years ago. Now I'll have her out to me before the autumn. What day is he sailing?

AUNT ELLEN.

Don't mind what the people are saying Donough. There's not a word of truth in it all.

DONOUGH.

Isn't Denis going to Canada?

AUNT ELLEN.

He is, but not . . .

DONOUGH.

Well, then, what's to hinder me going along with him? 'Twill be a queer thing if he doesn't contrive to get me into a good job out there.

GEORGE.

He'll do nothing of the sort.

PETER.

Put the idea out of your head.

DONOUGH.

Why so?

DUFFY.

Listen here to me, Donough; I'll tell you the way it is. This family's too high up in themselves for the like of you or me. We're not class enough for them, do you see? The Geoghegans are a great people, the Duffys aren't good enough for them at all. We've been thrown over; Delia's not a fit match for my brave Denis. You'll be the next to go; it couldn't be expected that Jane Geoghegan would marry Donough Brosnan. They have plans of marrying Jane to a lord.

DONOUGH.

What's that you say?

GEORGE.

Don't mind him, Donough.

91

DONOUGH.

I will mind him.

GEORGE.

You can marry Jane to-morrow for all I care. Duffy's mad.

DUFFY.

Mad? Take care what you're saying, George Geoghegan. There's a law against slander and abuse as well as against breaking a promise of marriage. Here's my final word to you: Denis marries Delia and takes her with him to Canada.

GEORGE.

He can't.

DUFFY.

Or he finishes his course in Dublin and marries her when he's a doctor, the very minute he's qualified.

GEORGE.

He can't.

DUFFY.

Then I bring an action. £1,000 damages. You can take your choice. I'll give you ten

minutes to yourselves to talk it over. I've got
to go and see Magner for a minute. I'll be
back for an answer. Mind, I mean every word
I say. The marriage or an action. That's my
final word to you, you pack of schemers!

> [*He's off—what a slam he gave the
> door.*]

AUNT ELLEN.

He's a terrible man.

GEORGE.

That's a nice fix we're in.

PETER.

What the divil can we do now?

DONOUGH.

I don't understand what it's all about.

GEORGE.

We're kicking Denis out to Canada because
he's a useless, idle, extravagant fellow, and
Duffy has an idea that he's going out to some
big place there, and is mad he won't marry
Delia.

93

DONOUGH.

Is that the way it is? I never had much belief in Denis.

GEORGE.

I wish to God you could get Duffy and the rest to be of the same mind. There's no one in the village will believe the truth.

DONOUGH.

Sure, there's nothing harder to believe than the truth.

PETER.

But what are we going to do?

GEORGE.

Let me think. My head's bursting. What was it Duffy said? Either marry her and take her to Canada or go through with College, or else the breach of promise. . . . I won't send him back to College; I'd rather have the breach —'twouldn't cost me more in the end. Maybe Denis might be ten years in Dublin or twenty years missing his examinations and spending money. Oh, where would it all come from? . . . But £1,000 to go to Duffy, or £500 itself —we'd be ruined; we'd never get it back from the shop.

DONOUGH.

Yerra, let Duffy bring the case against Denis and bankrupt him. What matter?

GEORGE.

Bankrupt him! Do you think I'm the one to stand by and see a Geoghegan broken by a Duffy or anyone else? I'd sooner die in the Union. There's but the one thing for it. Denis must marry her; he must take her with him to Canada.

AUNT ELLEN.

He'll do that all right; sure he's mad to marry her.

GEORGE.

Call him down here, Peter.

AUNT ELLEN.

He's gone to bed I think.

GEORGE.

Pull him out of bed, then. This must be settled before Duffy comes back. He'll put the case into the lawyer's hands to-morrow if we don't.

PETER.

I'll call him. (*He's gone.*)

AUNT ELLEN.

It's a terrible upset we're in.

GEORGE.

It was all your fault with your schemes for saving the family's good name. If we'd told the truth from the first, this wouldn't be on us now. (*He's turning on her.*)

AUNT ELLEN.

That's a queer thing to say to me, George. Small respect you're showing me.

GEORGE.

I don't know what I'm saying.

AUNT ELLEN.

It looks like it indeed. Anyway, the truth's a dangerous thing to be saying in a little place like Ballycolman.

DONOUGH.

It will be all right. Denis will marry Delia, and there'll be no more about it.

GEORGE.

I won't have an easy minute till the pair of them are married and gone. Oh Donough, it's

96

an awful thing to be head of a family. Since the father died I've not had a minute's rest, pulled this way and that way, this one wanting to get married, another going into business, Baby flying up to Dublin, Denis doctoring— many a time I wished I was born an orphan.

AUNT ELLEN.

God forgive you.

GEORGE.

It's true, Aunt Ellen. Look at the life I've led between you all, and no one ever thinking maybe I'd want to get married, or have a bit of fun, or spend a bit of money. For two pins I'd throw the lot of ye over to-morrow and sail away out of this for ever.

AUNT ELLEN.

Yerra, talk sense, George; that's no way to be behaving.

GEORGE.

There's no escape for me. I'm caught like an old cow with her head in a stall.

[*Here's* PETER *back with* DENIS. *It was no lie saying he was in bed, look at his striped pyjamas and his elegant dressing gown.*]

DENIS.

What do you want me for? Haven't you bothered me enough this evening without hauling me out of bed?

GEORGE.

Denis, old Duffy has been here raging mad. He threatens a breach of promise unless you marry Delia. You'll have to do it. You'll have to marry her at once.

DENIS.

What? Marry Delia?

GEORGE.

Yes, and take her to Canada along with you.

DENIS.

Oh!

AUNT ELLEN.

I knew you'd be delighted. 'Twas breaking your heart parting from her.

DENIS.

And what are we to live on in Canada?

GEORGE.

You'll find plenty to live on.

98

AUNT ELLEN.

A man's lost without a woman out there, they say. You'd read on the papers the great scarcity of women there is in Canada.

PETER.

That's so; she'll be a great addition to you.

AUNT ELLEN.

Father Murphy would marry you to-morrow when he knows the hurry you're in.

DENIS.

I see. . . . Listen here to me. Haven't I agreed to everything you've planned for me all my life through. To-night I agreed to go to Canada because it's your wish; I agreed to break with Delia. Now you want me to take Delia off to Canada, without a position, without a place to go to, with a few pounds in my pocket that wouldn't keep us for a month. Put the idea out of your head; I'll not do it. There's things I'll submit to myself, but I won't ask Delia to share them.

GEORGE.

Do you mean to tell me you don't want to marry Delia? You don't care about her?

99

DENIS.

I do care for her. That's why I won't marry her.

GEORGE.

That's crazy talk. You'll do all right in Canada.

PETER.

You won't be there a week before you'll have a big position.

DONOUGH.

You're sure to do fine.

GEORGE.

A clever lad like you will get on fast.

DENIS.

You hadn't much opinion of my cleverness an hour ago. I'll have to rough it and take my chance with all the others, and as soon as I've made a place for myself I'll marry Delia; but I'll not ask her to share the roughness and poverty you're sending me out to.

GEORGE.

Denis, don't turn on us like this.

DENIS.

You turned on me bitterly to-night, George.
You've kicked me out, you've wrecked my life,
you've made me give up Delia.

GEORGE.

But I want you to marry her now.

DENIS.

And I won't.   You know why.

GEORGE.

I'd give you a few pounds going to Canada.

DENIS.

I won't take them.

GEORGE.

If you went back to College——

DENIS.

I won't go back to College.

AUNT ELLEN.

In the name of God, what do you want?

DENIS.

I want to be let make my own life in my own way. I want to be let alone and not bothered. (*He's going towards the door.*)

GEORGE.

Where are you off to?

DENIS.

To bed, of course—and to Canada.

GEORGE.

Will you marry Delia?

DENIS.

No. (*And he's gone.*)

DONOUGH.

Wait—Denis——(*He's gone after him.*)

[*Poor* GEORGE. *You'd have to pity him.*]

AUNT ELLEN.

And Duffy will be here in a minute for his answer.

PETER.

Well, it's the breach of promise now, and no mistake.

102

GEORGE

We're ruined, we're ruined!

AUNT ELLEN.

Yerra, not at all. Maybe when the fit of anger passes John Duffy will think better of what he said to-night. But we must stand up to him boldly; don't let on we're afraid of him.

PETER.

Maybe he'd come to terms.

GEORGE.

I wouldn't demean myself making terms with him. Let him bring us into the Courts. I'll face him; I'll not have it said I was afraid of him.

AUNT ELLEN.

That's right.

GEORGE.

A Geoghegan's as good as a Duffy any day.

AUNT ELLEN.

And better.

[*There's a knock.*]

Glory be to God! there he is.

103

PETER.

I suppose I'll have to let him in. 'Twouldn't do to pretend we're all gone to bed.

GEORGE.

I'm afraid of no man. Open the door. 'Tis terrible, oh, 'tis terrible! Why did I ever open my lips to-night about Denis? . . . I'm wondering . . . I'm wondering, Aunt, if you spoke to Duffy yourself to-night? You used to be good friends long ago, I've heard it said. I . . . I . . .

AUNT ELLEN.

To be sure I'll speak to him; a woman can often come around a man. Ye only heat him.

GEORGE.

I'll have nothing to do with compromises and settlements, and it's no surrender, as they say in Derry, but—but—do your best for me. Whisht! He's coming. I'll be up to speak to the mother.

[*And he slips out one door as* PETER *and* DUFFY *come in the other.*]

DUFFY.

Well, ma'am, I'm back. Where has George gone to?

AUNT ELLEN.

He slipped up to speak to his mother. Peter, go and look for him.

[*Isn't she cute the way she got rid of* PETER?]

Won't you sit down?

DUFFY.

I'd sooner stand. Two minutes will give me my answer, I suppose.

AUNT ELLEN.

Take it easy while you have a chance. . . . John Duffy, you're a clever man; I don't know a cleverer.

DUFFY.

I'm obliged for your good opinion, ma'am.

[*How stiff he is.*]

AUNT ELLEN.

That story of Denis being good for nothing is true, but it suits you not to believe it, and you're right. I'd do the same in your case.

DUFFY.

You would?

105

AUNT ELLEN.

I would so. Oh, I always gave in you were one of the smartest men in the country. . . . You're looking to getting a deal of money out of this action?

DUFFY.

I am.

AUNT ELLEN.

I wonder will you. They're queer, chancey, uncertain things, breach of promise cases. Great expense, a troop of lawyers, terrible harrying in the witness-box and maybe twenty pounds at the end of it all, or the case dismissed. And Delia such a nervous little girl, I wonder you'd like to drag her through the Courts.

DUFFY.

Don't be afraid for Delia ma'am. A thousand pounds will cover a deal of blushes.

AUNT ELLEN.

A thousand pounds! You'll never see the quarter of it, no, nor a hundred pounds. It's the foolish people who go looking for money in a breach of promise case. The wise ones settle it up between themselves—and you were never a foolish man, Mr. Duffy.

106

Duffy.

I'm foolish enough, anyway, not to let my name be trampled in the dirt. It doesn't suit me to have Delia treated as if she wasn't good enough for a Geoghegan.

Aunt Ellen.

'Tis a pity. She'll hardly get married so. The lads are shy of having anything to say to a girl was in a breach of promise case —afraid they'd be the next to be hauled up. . . . What good will that do either of you? A little bit of money now slipped into your hand without bother or lawyers would be more value to you. A clever man would settle the whole thing for fifty pounds.

Duffy.

Would he indeed?

Aunt Ellen.

You know well the Geoghegans are a weak family. If you got a couple of hundred pounds damages itself, who knows would you ever be paid? But it doesn't reflect well on me to have my nephews dragged into Court. Come, Mr. Duffy, if I gave you fifty pounds would you withdraw the case?

DUFFY.

I've got my senses still, thank God. Fifty pounds? Keep it.

AUNT ELLEN.

That's not a civil way to be answering me—and yet we were good friends once—John.

DUFFY.

We were.

AUNT ELLEN.

I often think of those old days—ah, I suppose you've forgotten them long ago. But we were good friends.

DUFFY.

'Twasn't my fault we weren't closer than friends.

> [*After all, he's sitting down and near her too.*]

AUNT ELLEN.

I remember. Those days are gone long ago. . . . You'd have given me anything I asked, then.

DUFFY.

I would.

108

AUNT ELLEN.

Do you remember the day you walked twelve miles to get a red ribbon I'd set my mind on having for the races?

DUFFY.

I do.

AUNT ELLEN.

And now I'm offering you fifty pounds, and you throw it back in my face as if I was an old hen-woman at a fair.

DUFFY.

Fifty pounds is no money at all.

AUNT ELLEN.

Sixty, then . . . seventy . . . Ah, John, you couldn't refuse me. . . . for the sake of old times . .

DUFFY.

A lot your talking of old times. Look here, Ellen, are you in earnest? Do you want the case stopped?

AUNT ELLEN.

I do so.

DUFFY.

Then there's a way you can do it.

AUNT ELLEN.

Tell it to me.

DUFFY.

You can do what I asked you to do when we were boy and girl together.

AUNT ELLEN.

Mr. Duffy!

DUFFY.

Why not? Give me a hundred pounds down, and promise me you'll marry me before Shrove, and I'll let Denis and the Geoghegans go to the divil.

AUNT ELLEN.

I could never do it.

DUFFY.

You were near doing it fifteen years ago, after I buried the wife.

AUNT ELLEN.

I've lived my own life always, I'm too old to change. I wanted freedom. I wanted to

110

live like the birds, I wanted to do what I pleased with my own money.

DUFFY.

You've had your freedom, and what have you made out of it? Nothing at all. You've run after crazy schemes, goats and the like; your farm is gone to waste; you're getting on in years, soon you'll be an old woman, Ellen, with no one to look after you, only relations craving for your money. You'd better have me; I'll take care of you, I'll look after you, you'll have all the freedom you want. When you were a girl, Ellen, you were too proud to look at me, and I married Honora Reilly to spite you. After she died on me I asked you again, but you wouldn't have me. You're the only woman I ever wanted. You made me mad to-night with your talk of old times. You must marry me, you must! Never will you regret it . . .

AUNT ELLEN.

I couldn't, John. I'm old. I'd like to be free.

DUFFY.

Good-night, so.

AUNT ELLEN.

Why are you going?

111

DUFFY.

What use is there in me staying?

AUNT ELLEN

But what about the case?

DUFFY.

I'll see the lawyer in the morning.

AUNT ELLEN.

You're a hard man. You always get what you want.

DUFFY.

I didn't get the one thing I wanted in all the world.

AUNT ELLEN.

If I gave you a hundred pounds without the promise?

DUFFY.

'Twouldn't do me

AUNT ELLEN.

Why do you want to marry me?

DUFFY.

Contrariness, I suppose.

[*He's kissed her, glory be to God!*]
112

AUNT ELLEN.

Stop, John! You should be ashamed of yourself.

DUFFY.

You'll have me. I see you will.

AUNT ELLEN.

You're taking a lot for granted.

DUFFY.

I'm taking you, anyway. (*He's kissed her again!*)

AUNT ELLEN.

You're a terrible man.

DUFFY.

Why the divil didn't you let me do that thirty years ago, when we were boy and girl together? I made an offer at it one time, and you slapped me across the face.

AUNT ELLEN.

It's what I'd like to do to you this minute.

DUFFY.

You may then. (*Look at him sticking his face out to her.*)

AUNT ELLEN.

Get along with you!

DUFFY.

Cripes! I'd like to get drunk, I'd like to pull the house down, I'd like to go bawling singing through the streets of Ballycolman!

AUNT ELLEN.

I hope you'll do nothing of the kind, a respectable man like you, with a grown daughter and a wife interred.

DUFFY.

Don't remind me of her. I'm twenty years old—not a minute more.

AUNT ELLEN.

If you keep shouting like that you'll have George down.

DUFFY.

Faith, that reminds me . . . I'll draw up a paper and you can sign it. (*He's always an eye to business.*)

114

AUNT ELLEN.

What are you asking me to sign?

DUFFY

A promise to pay me a hundred pounds down, and that you'll marry me before Shrove provided I drop the case against Denis . . . Have you your cheque-book handy?

AUNT ELLEN.

It's here in my bag.

DUFFY.

Make out a cheque so for me for a hundred pounds.

AUNT ELLEN.

It's a whip of money.

DUFFY.

Sure, it's not going to pass out of the family. I'll spend it on stocking the farm.

AUNT ELLEN.

You're a terrible man . . . I suppose you must have your way. (*She's writing him a cheque, it must be a fact that she's in love with him.*)

115

DUFFY.

Sign there, now.

[*She's doing that too. He's got the cheque and the paper signed and into his breast pocket they go.*]

AUNT ELLEN.

For the love of goodness don't breathe a word of this to the Geoghegans. They'd have my life for making terms with you. I'll find my own way later of telling them about the marriage.

DUFFY.

I'll not open my lips. And it would suit me better if they thought I withdrew the case of my own free will. Isn't it like a story on the pictures, Ellen, the way you and I have come together at the end of all. (*More love-making. Look at his arm around her waist.*)

AUNT ELLEN.

Leave go of me; there's someone coming.

[*It's* GEORGE, *and his Aunt's slipped out. She's all in a flutter and no wonder.*]

GEORGE.

I'm sorry for leaving you so long, Mr. Duffy. I was speaking to my mother and that

116

young rascal of a brother of mine. It's no use trying to make him see reason; you might as well be talking to a deaf man.

DUFFY.

Is that so?

GEORGE.

My aunt was speaking to you?

DUFFY.

She was.

GEORGE.

I hope you're feeling in a more reasonable way?

DUFFY.

Oh, I've reason on my side.

GEORGE.

There's no use expecting Denis to marry Delia; he'll not do it. What we've got to do, Mr. Duffy, is to settle our little difference the best way we can.

DUFFY.

That's a fact.

117

GEORGE.

I'm glad to see you taking that view. What use is there going into Court? Five minutes friendly talk is better than all the lawyers in the Four Courts . . . Come, John, we were always good friends—what will you take to drop the case?

DUFFY.

To . . . ? Five hundred pounds. (*Tch! Tch!*)

GEORGE.

I mean in earnest.

DUFFY.

I'm speaking in earnest.

GEORGE.

I'll give you two hundred.

DUFFY.

Put your hand there. There's one condition I make : not one word of this to your family, or anyone. I'd rather have it thought that I withdrew the case myself.

GEORGE.

It will suit me, too, to be quiet about this. The family would be mad with me for going

118

behind their backs. My aunt was all for fight-
ing you to the bitter end.

DUFFY.

Was she indeed?

GEORGE.

Don't mind a word she was saying; she's a
cranky old schemer.

DUFFY.

Would you believe me telling you she came
near striking me to-night?

GEORGE.

She did? Don't mind her, John; she didn't
mean a word she said.

DUFFY.

Faith, there's things she said to-night I'll
hold her accountable for . . . Tell me, when
will you let me have the money?

GEORGE.

I'll write a letter to you to-night promising
to pay it in six months' time, provided you
don't bring up the case. I'll have to look about
for the money.

DUFFY.

That'll do me. But if I haven't the letter in the morning I'll start with the case.

GEORGE.

Oh, you'll have it, never fear.

[*Here's poor* MRS. GEOGHEGAN.]

MRS. GEOG.

Is that Mr. Duffy's voice?

DUFFY.

Good-night to you ma'am.

MRS. GEOG.

Is it true what I hear that you're making a set against my poor Denis, that you're going to bring him into the Courts?

DUFFY.

That's so.

GEORGE.

Don't go into it now, mother. I've been talking it over with Mr. Duffy. By to-morrow morning he's likely to see matters in a more reasonable way.

120

DUFFY.

I'm a generous man, ma'am.   (*You are!*)

MRS. GEOG.

I know you are.   I'll say no more, only
leave it to God and yourself . . . Would you
oblige me by taking a note down to Delia?

DUFFY.

Certainly, ma'am.

GEORGE.

What's that, mother?

MRS. GEOG.

Only a letter of good-bye from my poor
Denis.   There's a note for yourself, too, Mr.
Duffy.

> [*She's half-whispering, she doesn't
> want* GEORGE *to hear, but he's writing the
> note to* DUFFY *in the corner of the room.*]

DUFFY.

Thank you, ma'am.   (*It's a thick letter; he
can't help himself from opening it.*)

MRS. GEOG.

Are you going to bed, George?

GEORGE.

I have to write one letter first.

[*Look what* DUFFY'S *pulling out of the envelope. Notes! Bank notes.......!*]

DUFFY.

. . . May the divil . . .

MRS. GEOG.

What's the matter, Mr. Duffy? (*She's afraid* GEORGE *will notice and her finger's on her lips.*)

DUFFY.

Oh, nothing at all, ma'am, nothing at all. I'll be going.

MRS. GEOG.

I hope business is good by you these times?

DUFFY.

Business? Oh, business, ma'am is good; never better, never better. Well, be the . . . Good-night to you both.

[*He's gone. Well, well, such strategy and manœuvring—such lying as you might call it.*]

CURTAIN.

Act III

[*The scene is the same but it's morning and* Baby *singing at the piano . . . Yes, a lovely voice, 'twas the nuns taught her. . . . What's that she's singing? "Because God Made you Mine," one of them religious songs I suppose. Look at poor* Kate *dusting the room. She's no singer.*]

Kate.

That's lovely, Baby. You've a great turn for music.

Baby.

I have, then. I love them passionate songs. There's some like comics, but give me a song with passion in it. It goes through me like. I suppose I'm queer.

Kate.

Why wouldn't you like them? Myself, I could never tell one tune from another, but I'd listen to you all day.

BABY.

Whisper here, Kate. I had a letter from Maggie Clancy this morning, from Dublin. She wants me to go up to her before Christmas.

KATE.

And will you?

BABY.

I will so. Then I'll be able to start at the classes the very minute Christmas is over.

KATE.

Where'll you get the money?

BABY.

George got twenty pound for sheep yesterday; the money's upstairs. He's promised it to me; and maybe I could coax a few pounds out of mother.

KATE.

I suppose you're longing to be off.

BABY.

God knows there's wings in my heart to be gone out of this. I could never stay on here the way you did, never seeing a bit of life or

124

having a chance . . . Are you sorry you didn't get married that time?

KATE.

Oh, Babe, often I lie awake thinking of it. Not that we were such friends; twice only I saw him; but he was a big, powerful, hairy man, and to have a place of my own and not to be depending always on other people—even though they're your own family.

BABY.

I know, I know; 'tis hard on you. Maybe you'll get a chance of marrying again.

KATE.

Yerra, no; I'm too old. Ah, where's the use in talking of it?

[*Here's the mother.*]

MRS. GEOG.

Have either of you seen Denis?

BABY.

We didn't.

KATE.

I gave him a bit of breakfast very early— 'twasn't more than half-seven, I think, and he went out and I didn't lay eyes on him since.

MRS. GEOG.

And now it's close on twelve o'clock! Oh, Kate, do you think is there anything after happening to him?

KATE.

Yerra, what would happen to him?

MRS. GEOG.

What mightn't happen after all the work there was last night? Shipped off to Canada, parted from the girl he loves, many a man has thrown himself into the river for less.

KATE.

Ah, not at all.

BABY.

There was a grand song I used to sing one time about a girl drowned herself for love, but I've never had a song about a man destroying himself for a girl. Anyway, Denis is the sort takes good care of himself. You needn't fret about him.

MRS. GEOG.

God grant you're right. But all the same I wish you'd walk up street and see is there ere a sign of him.

126

BABY.

I might do that. Listen here, mother. I'm off to Dublin in a day or two.

MRS. GEOG.

You are?

BABY.

I'll want clothes and the like, going to Dublin. I suppose you won't grudge giving me a bit of money?

MRS. GEOG.

Money? Where would I get money?

KATE.

Sure, the child would want a couple of pounds anyway.

BABY.

There's no need to be saving it for Denis any longer.

MRS. GEOG.

I see what's in your mind the same as if I was sitting inside you. You've grudged Denis every penny he ever got. The poor boy, he's no friend in the world but myself. Maybe he's lying cold and dead now by reason of the way he's been treated in this house by his own flesh and blood, but that's nothing at all to you so long as you can skeet out of this to Dublin. All his life it's been the same story: hindered at every turn, denied any little thing he had set his heart on, and for all that the cleverest of you all. I haven't got any money, and if I had it isn't to you I'd give it.

[*And with that, she's gone.*]

BABY.

If I wasn't so cross I'd want to laugh at the notion of us denying Denis anything!

KATE.

Well, we all treated him hardly enough last night.

BABY.

I believe you're soft on him still. I believe we all are in our hearts, only we daren't let on.

[*Here's* GEORGE.]

GEORGE.

Are you there, Baby? Did you take the money?

BABY.

I did not. Where is it?

128

GEORGE.

In my box. At least it was; it's not there now.

BABY.

Do you mean it's stolen?

GEORGE.

Ah, who'd steal it? I must have put it in some other place. But it's queer. I'm certain it was there I put it. I'll have another look.

[*He's gone again. Aren't they a worry to him the whole flock of them.*]

BABY.

'Twould be a nice thing if, after all, the money was gone.

KATE.

George brought it down to the shop maybe.

[JANE'S *coming in now and a paper in her hand.*]

JANE.

You're after vexing the mother with your talk of going to Dublin.

9   129

Baby.

Why should it vex her? She was wild for Denis to go, and now she's mad with me for following his example.

Jane.

Of course a boy is different . . . You've your mind made up?

Baby.

I'm off a Monday, if I can get the money.

Jane.

Monday! I wish you'd wait and see me married. I ran across to Peg Turpin's this morning for a minute. She lent me this. Look here; it's full of the queerest, grandest things ever you saw.

Baby.

Is it *Weldon's* you have?

Jane.

No. A better paper—*V o g u e*. Peg's sister sent it her from Dublin.

[*Tch, tch! Look at them all round it like wasps round a jam-pot.*]

What would you think of that one?

130

BABY.

To be married in?

JANE.

Yes.

KATE.

Wouldn't you feel ashamed-like walking up the chapel in it?

JANE.

I would not.

BABY.

It's elegant, elegant! That now with tan shoes and white gloves—only I don't like the hat. 'Tis too quiet for a wedding. You should have something flashier—a big feather, or one of them scarlet seagulls.

KATE.

For God's sake look over the page.

BABY.

Well, of all the . . . !

JANE.

It's extraordinary the things they put in those fashion papers.

KATE.

I'd drop dead if I had that on me.

BABY.

It's not so outlandish when you've looked at it for a while. "This simple, girlish frock" —that's what's written under it. It should suit me, so. Would you fancy me in it?

KATE.

You'd look lovely in anything, Babe. But I'd be in dread Father Murphy would speak of it from the altar if you paraded Ballycolman in that rig-out.

BABY.

Do you think I'd waste it on Ballycolman? It's in Dublin I'd wear it.

JANE.

There's a blouse below at Peg's I've set my heart on. 'Tis lace from here to here, stripes of green velvet, gold buttons—oh, 'tis gorgeous!

[*Here's* AUNT ELLEN.]

AUNT ELLEN.

Is there no sign of Denis?

132

JANE.

He's not been here. I hope to goodness nothing's happened to him.

BABY.

You're as bad as mother. She has him killed and buried . . . Look, Aunt, what would you think of me in that?

AUNT ELLEN.

Show . . . Wisha, Babe, you'd never disgrace us going about like that!

BABY.

It's elegant. And Jane has a lovely one here picked for her wedding.

AUNT ELLEN.

Are there wedding dresses there? Show me.

BABY.

I believe Aunt Ellen is thinking of getting married!

[*Listen to them all laughing.*]

AUNT ELLEN.

How smart you are! . . . What about that one, girls? Supposing—supposing I was getting married.

133

Baby.

Sure, that's a opera cloak, Aunt.

[*Look at* Duffy *coming in.   He's looking   pleased   with   himself.*]

Duffy.

Good-morning to you.

Baby.

Good-morning, Mr. Duffy.

Jane.

Good-morning, Mr. Duffy.

Kate.

Good-morning, Mr. Duffy.

Duffy.

Good-morning, Ellen.   I hope you're good.

Aunt Ellen.

I am, thank you.

Duffy.

Were you thinking over what I said to you last night?

134

AUNT ELLEN.

To tell you the truth, I never thought of it since.

[*God forgive her!*]

DUFFY.

You didn't?

AUNT ELLEN.

Never once.

BABY.

Her mind's full of the one thing only at the present minute, Mr. Duffy—dresses, wedding dresses, no less. It's my belief she's going to get married on the sly.

AUNT ELLEN.

Hold your tongue.

DUFFY.

Wedding dresses? Is that what you're at? Oh, that's all right . . . However, I didn't come here to talk the fashions; I wanted to see George for a minute.

KATE.

He's above. I'll call him.

135

JANE.

Come on across to Peg's, Babe, till you see the blouse I was telling you about.

[*The three of them are off with themselves. They'll spend the rest of the morning talking fashions at Peg's.*]

DUFFY.

So you've fixed on the dress already?

AUNT ELLEN.

I haven't. But if I've got to be married, I may as well be married decently.

DUFFY.

Oh, never fear, we'll make a smart thing of it . . . Do you know, Ellen, Easter's terrible late this year.

AUNT ELLEN.

Is it? But what matter? I always think it's nicer late.

DUFFY.

But a late Easter makes a late Shrove. I looked at the calendar before I slept last night. Holy Star, I could hardly believe my eyes. I don't think there was ever such a late Easter in the memory of man.

AUNT ELLEN.

What matter?

DUFFY.

Christmas, I'd have said if I'd known; and I think Christmas it must be, Ellen.

AUNT ELLEN.

What? Marry you before Christmas? I'll do no such thing.

DUFFY.

I can't wait. You must.

AUNT ELLEN.

I tell you, you must wait.

DUFFY.

Peg will make you a dress in a week . . . If you won't, I'll have to tell George about the bargain you made.

AUNT ELLEN.

You wouldn't do such a thing after you promising.

DUFFY.

A man in love, you know . . .

[*Here's* GEORGE *and the mother.*]

Mrs. Geog.

Mr. Duffy, did you see Denis?

Duffy.

I didn't. He wasn't over at my place. Delia's in bed, sick.

Mrs. Geog.

The creature! . . . I hope, Mr. Duffy, you've come up to tell us you've changed your mind about the breach of promise? I'm sure you couldn't wish to be hard on us, old friends as we are.

George.

To be sure, Mr. Duffy will be reasonable.

Aunt Ellen.

You're all talking as if the man was something terrible.

Duffy.

Well, I've been thinking things over . . . I've a strong case to go on, there's no one can say I haven't. I've justice on my side, my good name to keep up, the honour of my poor motherless girl, and—and all that. But, after all, quarrelling among neighbours is a bad thing. Your poor father, George, was a good

138

friend of mine, and for his sake, and because it's Delia's wish, and because I'm a peaceable Christian man, I'm going to withdraw the case.

MRS. GEOG.

The blessing of God on you for that word!

GEORGE.

Thank you, John.

DUFFY.

Mind you, it's a great loss to me. I'm letting a deal of money go from me, and I suppose there'll be people who'll say behind my back— aye, and up to my puss, maybe—that the Geoghegans bested the Duffys. But I don't care. I'll bear all that for the sake of the good-will I have to the family.

MRS. GEOG.

You won't be without your reward.

GEORGE.

Shake hands, John. You've spoken like a man.

MRS. GEOG.

If ever I wronged you in my thoughts, Mr. Duffy, may God forgive me and reward you as you deserve.

DUFFY.

I'm looking for nothing ma'am. I'm glad I was able to do this for you. And now I must be going back to the Post Office. The Inspector might be here this morning.

GEORGE.

Wouldn't you have something before you go?

DUFFY.

No, thank you, George. Seldom I touch anything.

GEORGE.

Ah, a small drop . . . Come, John?

DUFFY.

Well, just a mouthful.

GEORGE.

A drop for you, Aunt?

AUNT ELLEN.

No, thank you, George.

GEORGE.

You're like myself; you touch nothing. You'll have some, mother?

140

MRS. GEOG.

A small drop—for Mr. Duffy's sake. Here's long life to you, Mr. Duffy.

DUFFY.

Well, here's luck to . . .

[*It would make you thirsty to watch them. Would we have time to slip out for a——Whisht! Here's* DENIS *and* DELIA.]

MRS. GEOG.

Denis! Where were you? I thought you were gone from us.

DENIS.

Not at all. You don't get rid of me quite as easily as that. Good-morning, Mr. Duffy.

DUFFY.

Morning.

MRS. GEOG.

Sit down, Delia. Would you take a glass of wine?

DELIA.

No, thank you, Mrs. Geoghegan.

141

DENIS.

You might as well. Drink success to me in Canada, and all that sort of thing.

DELIA.

Oh, I'll do that.

[*They're all trying to make up to her.*]

MRS. GEOG.

Don't fret over this, alanna. It will all come right in the end, I'm sure. Maybe in a year or two Denis will be able to come back and marry you.

DUFFY.

I thought you were sick.

DELIA.

I'm better.

DUFFY.

You look it.

DELIA.

You seem sorry.

DUFFY.

You'd better come along home now. The Inspector's likely to come this morning, and 'tis

142

you know about them postal orders that went astray on us.

DELIA.

I'll come in a minute.

MRS. GEOG.

She wants to see a little of Denis before he goes, small blame to her.

DUFFY.

Ay, he'll have other things to do in future besides love-making.

DELIA.

Indeed, yes. I suppose, Denis, our love-making has come to an end?

DUFFY.

That's a sensible girl. I thought maybe you'd be for not giving him up.

GEORGE.

I'm sorry, Delia, we had to come between the two of you, but there was nothing else for it.

DELIA.

I'm sure you only did what was right, George.

143

DENIS.

As a matter of fact, I haven't given Delia up.

DUFFY.

But you must.

GEORGE.

You can't get married, you know.

AUNT ELLEN.

You're off to Canada to-morrow.

DENIS.

Yes, yes, I know all that. George, I've been thinking things over. What you said last night was true. I've been a bad brother to you, it's right for you to turn me out. The only thing that makes me unhappy is the case that Mr. Duffy threatens against us.

GEORGE.

That needn't bother you.

DENIS.

It does. It's likely to draw a lot of money out of you.

GEORGE.

Hush! Listen here . . .

144

DENIS.

All my life through I've sacrificed myself to
you; I've done all you wished me to; I'll go
through with it to the end. Forgive me for
what I said last night. I've seen I was wrong.
I wrote another letter to Delia last night; I
saw her early this morning, and we talked the
matter over. Don't let the weight of the
breach of promise be on your mind a minute
longer. Mr. Duffy will never bring it.

DUFFY.

How do you know I won't, young man?

DENIS.

Because, Mr. Duffy, Delia and I were
married half an hour ago.

[*Well, glory be to God!*]

DUFFY.

Ye . . . ? It's a lie.

DENIS.

I beg your pardon; it's true.

DUFFY.

You couldn't be married so smart.

DENIS.

Father Murphy had heard the story of my
going to Canada, and he was quite ready to
marry me. I'm so glad, George, I've done
what you wished me to do . . . Excuse me
for a few minutes.

[*He's gone out. Where's he gone to?*]

DUFFY.

How dare you—how dare you!

[*He's in a temper. No wonder.*]

DELIA.

Father!

DUFFY.

Ruining me—ruining me, that's what you'd
like to be doing. Hadn't I my fortune made?
Wasn't I settled for life? Look at here! A
letter from George giving me two hundred
pounds provided I don't go on with the case.

MRS. GEOG.

George!

AUNT ELLEN

George, how could you!

GEORGE.

I didn't, I didn't!

146

DUFFY.

Look at here again—twenty pounds in notes from Mrs. Geoghegan to let the case drop, to put nothing in the way of the two of you.

GEORGE.

That's the twenty pounds I missed this morning. Give them here; they're mine.

AUNT ELLEN.

Ann, I'm surprised at you!

DUFFY.

And look at this. A hundred pounds from Aunt Ellen and a promise to marry me before Shrove. And now I suppose it's no better than waste paper.

MRS. GEOG.

Ellen, I'm amazed at you, thinking of getting married at your age!

GEORGE.

Aunt Ellen, after what you said!

DELIA.

Quiet yourself, father.

147

DUFFY.

'Tis easy to say, "Quiet yourself!" I never thought you'd turn on me like that, Delia—the only child I ever had!

DELIA.

Sure, it's pleasing you I thought we'd be. Last night you were fit to be tied at the notion of my not getting married.

DUFFY.

I thought I had spirit enough to throw you over. But the Geoghegans are a mean-spirited lot; they haven't even the courage to jilt a girl.

AUNT ELLEN.

Well, thank God, I'm free of my promise and have courage enough to jilt you, Mr. Duffy.

[*There's a stab!*]

DUFFY.

Do you hear what she says, Delia? That's your doing . . . I've your hundred pounds, anyway, and I'll not give it up, not if you bring me into a court of law. And I've your twenty pounds in notes, ma'am; I'll not part with them.

GEORGE.

They're not hers; they're mine.

DUFFY.

Faith, they're mine now.

GEORGE.

For Baby they were meant. Do you know, mother, I could have you put in jail for a thief?

MRS. GEOG.

And what about the two hundred pounds you squandered unknown to any of us?

GEORGE.

And you, Aunt Ellen, after all you said about putting a bold face on it, no surrender, and the like . . .

MRS. GEOG.

Yes, indeed, you were very brazen, engaging yourself to be married like that!

GEORGE.

Look here, Mr. Duffy, give me back that letter I wrote to you.

DUFFY.

I will not.

AUNT ELLEN.

Give me back my cheque.

MRS. GEOG.

I'd be thankful for that twenty pounds.

DUFFY.

There's been trickery and underhand dealing here. I'm not inclined to part with these in a hurry.

GEORGE.

Trickery? Underhand dealing? You're a nice one to talk of trickery when you had us all tricked up to the eyes last night, and making me promise not to say a word of it to anyone! And I suppose you had Aunt Ellen bound the same way. And mother robbing me, and Aunt Ellen betraying me behind my back— Is it thieves and traitors I'm dealing with?

AUNT ELLEN.

And what about yourself, George?

DELIA.

Look here, all of you, what's the use going on like this, scolding and attacking each other? Too smart you've all been trying to be, and Denis and I have shown you up. Can't you make peace now? Can't you . . .

150

Duffy.

Will you hold your tongue, girl! Enough trouble you've made already. One certain thing is—after this morning's work I'm done with you—done with you. You can leave the house to-day; not a shilling will you ever get from me.

George.

And I say the same about Denis. We're quit of him now for ever. I tell you it's very soon, Delia, you'll repent of the deceitful way you acted to-day.

Delia.

You can spare your words, George, and you, too, father. Denis and I aren't asking help from any of you. We can get on very well without you. Denis has got work; he can support his wife, and no thanks to any of you.

Duffy.

Is he after getting an appointment?

Mrs. Geog.

I knew something good would turn up for him.

George.

What is it, Delia?

DELIA.

Here he is himself; he'll tell you.

[*In the name of goodness will you look
at him! 'Tis overalls he has on him and
his trousers tied with string and a muffler
round his neck and an old greasy cap.
What at all can have happened?*]

MRS. GEOG.

For goodness sake! Denis!

AUNT ELLEN.

Where in God's name did you get the
clothes?

DENIS.

Larry Hogan lent me them.

DELIA.

I've been telling them, Denis, that you've got
work. Tell them what it is.

DENIS.

I haven't much time. I want a bite of something before I go. (*He's looking at his wrist
watch.*) I'm due in ten minutes. By the way,
you might keep this watch, Delia; it's hardly
suitable to my employment.

[*He gives it to he*r.]
152

GEORGE.

Where are you going?

DENIS.

Oh, not far; don't fret, George; not as far as Canada; not farther, in fact, than a hundred yards from the shop door.

GEORGE.

What do you mean?

DENIS.

Well, as we came up the street from the chapel after being married one of the men working on the road where the steam-roller is was taken ill. I saw he was pretty bad and ordered him off to hospital. The foreman was cursing at being left short-handed; I offered myself in the sick man's place. I'm to go down there after dinner hour at one o'clock . . .

[*What the*——*!*]

Delia is going to see if we can get two rooms in one of Nolan's cottages. I'll send up for my clothes this evening. You'll be glad to see me starting to work at last, George.

GEORGE.

You're—you're mad.

153

DUFFY.

You'll be working on the street?

DENIS.

Yes, on the street. I hope in a day or two we'll have worked up as far as the Post Office, Mr. Duffy.

DUFFY.

Oh, my God!

MRS. GEOG.

Denis, Denis, you mustn't do it! George, speak to him, speak to him!

GEORGE.

Denis, boy, don't do it. Hard as we were on you, we wouldn't like to drive you to that.

DENIS.

My dear old chap, don't worry about me. I assure you, I don't mind. Ballycolman or Canada, it's all the same to me. In fact, I prefer Ballycolman. I like being amongst friends.

GEORGE.

Friends! Think what everyone will say of you, and what sort of a name will they put on us to say we drove you out on the road!

154

DENIS.

Oh, let them say what they like. Mother, give me a bit of bread and a drink of milk. I must be off, or I'll lose my job. And you might put some tea in a can.

MRS. GEOG.

I'll not. You to be working, Denis! It's a disgrace we'd never get over.

DUFFY.

Delia, speak to him; make him hear reason.

DELIA.

Why should I? You told me straight a minute ago we needn't look to you for help. We've got to live. Do you think Nolan's have a room.

DUFFY.

Delia, Delia, do you want to break my heart? A Duffy to be in one of Nolan's little houses! Look at here—let the two of you come and live with me.

[*He's almost crying.*]

GEORGE.

Come and live here.

155

Aunt Ellen.

Come and live out at my place.

Denis.

No, thanks. I want to be independent. I want to be working.

George.

We'd get you something decent to do.

Duffy.

A job will turn up for you. Amn't I Chairman of the District Council? I'm sure you know enough doctoring to be a tuberculosis officer . . . or . . .

Denis.

No, I don't.

George.

Think of something, Aunt Ellen. You were always a woman for schemes.

Aunt Ellen.

Denis, I always favoured you; you were always my pet. Come out to Kilmurray; manage the shop there. It's a hundred and fifty a year in your pocket, and I'll leave you the farm when I die.

156

DUFFY.

Do, Denis!

MRS. GEOG.

Do, like a good boy.

GEORGE.

For the mother's sake.

AUNT ELLEN.

Don't be pussy with us, Denis.

[*Look at him smiling and shaking his head.*]

DUFFY.

Look at here: I'll give you this if you will. There's twenty pounds.

DENIS.

Keep it, Mr. Duffy.

DUFFY.

Here's your aunt's cheque for £100—'tis endorsed and all.

AUNT ELLEN.

Take it, Denis, take it.

157

DUFFY.

George, will you give him that £200?

GEORGE.

I will.   Anything to save us from this.

DENIS.

I don't want it.

DUFFY.

Then what in the earthly world will tempt
you?

DENIS.

I only want to be able to do what I like with
my own life—to be free.

DUFFY.

Free? . . .   Bedad, isn't he like old Ireland
asking for freedom, and we're like the fools
of Englishmen offering him every bloody thing
except the one thing? . . .   Do Denis, do like
a darling boy, go out to Kilmurray and manage
the shop.

DENIS.

I don't know that much about shop-keeping.
158

GEORGE.

Yerra, that's the best reason you could have for going. Sure, 'tisn't a real shop, only one of them co-operatives. The sooner it bursts the better.

DENIS.

You'd like to force me to do this just the way you forced me to do everything else—to go to Dublin, to go to Canada, to give up Delia. Will I never be free from you? . . . If I go —but mind you, I don't say I will—Delia will have to look after the shop. I won't.

DUFFY.

Now, Delia, be a good girl; say you will.

DELIA.

Denis, we're beaten; we'll have to go, we'll have to give in to them. But don't fret yourself; I'll look after the shop; you'll never be asked to do a hand's turn in it.

GEORGE.

God bless you, Delia.

DELIA.

Listen here, George. Don't flatter yourself that shop's going to fail. It's not. It's going to best you all—you can make up your mind to that.

GEORGE.

Begob, I wouldn't wonder if it would, with you at the head of it.

DUFFY.

Isn't she a Duffy?

DELIA.

There's not one of you here have ever understood Denis. He's been straitened and denied all his life through, but I'm going to give him what he wants now.

DENIS

Do you think Kilmurray is what I want?

DELIA.

An easy life, no responsibility, money in your pocket, something to grumble at— What more do you want?

AUNT ELLEN.

Maybe we'll get you something better later on, Denis. And anyway you'll have the farm when I die.

DUFFY.

Ellen Geoghegan, what sort is the farm likely to be the day you die, and you treating it the way you do? Listen here: isn't it your sacred and solemn duty to those two helpless young creatures to take care you leave it to them in good condition?

[*That's right.*]

AUNT ELLEN.

Maybe so.

DUFFY.

To do that you've got to marry me.

AUNT ELLEN.

I'm free of my promise; I'd rather keep free.

DUFFY.

You daren't. Not with the responsibility that's on you now. Suppose you squandered the farm?

AUNT ELLEN.

You frighten me! I suppose, for Denis's sake, I'll have to have you so.

DUFFY.

That's the woman! And maybe in the end of all you won't get the farm, Denis, my boy.

11   161

AUNT ELLEN.

What are you saying?

DUFFY.

What's to hinder us having a son of our own?

AUNT ELLEN.

Mr. Duffy, I'm surprised at you. I didn't think you could be so coarse.

[. . . *Yes, she have a very delicate mind.*]

DUFFY.

I'm sorry, Ellen; I'm sorry. Still you never know what mightn't happen.

MRS. GEOG.

Ellen, if that day ever comes to you,—and I pray that it will,—take my advice, go up to Dublin and see Sir Denis. He's an old man, but he's hearty yet, I'm told, and . . .

DUFFY.

No, no, ma'am. One whiteheaded boy is as much as this family can support. We're not going to rear another.

162

MRS. GEOG.

Well, thank God, everything's well settled.
I'm dying to tell the others; they'll be delighted.

GEORGE.

Begob, I clean forgot them!

AUNT ELLEN.

Peter will have to stay on here.

GEORGE.

Jane can't get married.

AUNT ELLEN.

Baby can't go to Dublin.

GEORGE.

How is it we all forgot them?

AUNT ELLEN.

Thinking all the time of Denis we were.

GEORGE.

What in hell are we to do? . . . There's
a noise in the street . . . It's them coming.
. . . What are we to say to them? They'll
have my life.

Mrs. Geog.

Quiet yourself, George. They'll be all delighted when they hear the way Denis is settled for life. I'll talk to them. Leave it to me.

George.

Faith, I'll do that with a heart and a half. I'll see you later, John.

[*He's glad to go.*]

Mrs. Geog.

Don't take it hardly Denis. There are worse things than a shop and a farm and £320 in your hand, and when all's said and done it's better than working on the roads.

Denis.

I'm not going to grumble, mother, where's the use? I've always had to do what you all made me do, and I suppose I may as well go on with it. I can't fight you all . . .

Mrs. Geog.

That's my brave darling boy. (*There's kissing!*) Oh, Delia, take care of him; he's not strong at all.

Delia.

I'll look after him. Give me the money, Denis, I'm going to put it in the bank. George must make me out a promissory note. While I'm at the bank, Denis, change your clothes. This afternoon we'll drive out to Kilmurray. I want to look at the shop.

[*That's the girl will manage him.* GEORGE *is sticking his head in the door.*]

GEORGE.

They're coming!

MRS. GEOG.

I'm ready for them.

[*Here's* KATE, JANE, BABY, DONOUGH *and* PETER, *all in together in great excitement; they all talking together.*]

ALL.

What's this we're after hearing—that Denis and Delia have got married?

BABY.

Is this a fact?

MRS. GEOG.

It's quite true, thanks be to God. Denis is married, he's going out to Kilmurray to manage the shop, we're after giving him £300 and more.

165

ALL.

What? What's that you say?

MRS. GEOG.

I knew you'd all be delighted.

ALL.

Delighted!

BABY.

I suppose this means I can't go to Dublin?

MRS. GEOG.

Not at all, you'll go—some day—never fear.

BABY.

Some day!

JANE.

Does this mean I can't marry Donough?

MRS. GEOG.

Not at all. You'll marry him—some day.

PETER.

And what about me?

Mrs. Geog.

You'll be all right—some day.

All.

Well, I think it's a shame.

Mrs. Geog.

Shame? Think shame to yourselves! What sort of unnatural children have I got at all? Would you grudge your brother the one little bit of luck he's had in all his life? Look at him sitting there with the girl he loves and he after marrying her and not one of you would as much as wish him joy.

Jane.

I'm sure, Denis, I have nothing against you. I hope you'll be happy only——

Baby.

May you be happy—s o m e d a y !

Peter.

Good luck to you.

Aunt Ellen.

Girls, look here. I've a plan in my mind for you all. After I'm married——

ALL.

After you're what?

[*They think she's mad.*]

DUFFY.

After w e ' r e married.

BABY.

That's the boldest plan she ever made. After you're married? Wisha, God help you, John Duffy.

[*And she's right.*]

CURTAIN.

The Whiteheaded Boy was first produced at the Abbey Theatre, Dublin, on December 13th, 1916, with the following cast:—

Mrs. Geoghegan	Eileen O'Doherty
George	Breffni O'Rourke
Peter	Arthur Shields
Kate	Dorothy Lynd
Baby	Maureen Delany
Jane	May Craig
Denis	Fred O'Donovan
Donough Brosnan	Peter Nolan
John Duffy	Chas. C. O'Reilly
Delia	Irene Kelly
Aunt Ellen	Maire O'Neill
Hannah	Sheila O'Sullivan

The play was produced by J. Augustus Keogh.

New Comedies

By
LADY GREGORY

The Bogie Men—The Full Moon—Coats
Damer's Gold—McDonough's Wife

8°. With Portrait in Photogravure

The plays have been acted with great success by the Abbey Company, and have been highly extolled by appreciative audiences and an enthusiastic press. They are distinguished by a humor of unchallenged originality.

One of the plays in the collection, "Coats," depends for its plot upon the rivalry of two editors, each of whom has written an obituary notice of the other. The dialogue is full of crisp humor. "McDonough's Wife," another drama that appears in the volume, is based on a legend, and explains how a whole town rendered honor against its will. "The Bogie Men" has as its underlying situation an amusing misunderstanding of two chimney-sweeps. The wit and absurdity of the dialogue are in Lady Gregory's best vein. "Damer's Gold" contains the story of a miser beset by his gold-hungry relations. Their hopes and plans are upset by one they had believed to be of the simple of the world, but who confounds the Wisdom of the Wise. "The Full Moon" presents a little comedy enacted on an Irish railway station. It is characterized by humor of an original and delightful character and repartee that is distinctly clever.

G. P. PUTNAM'S SONS

NEW YORK   **LONDON**

Irish Folk-History Plays

By

LADY GREGORY

Lady Gregory's plays "never fail to do the one thing which we all demand from a play, which is not, as stupid people say, to amuse us (though Lady Gregory's plays are extremely amusing), but to take us out of ourselves and out of London and out of the stuffy theater while we are listening to them."—*George Bernard Shaw.*

"Among the three great exponents of the modern Celtic movement in Ireland, Lady Gregory holds an unusual place. It is she from whom came the chief historical impulse which resulted in the re-creation for the present generation of the elemental poetry of early Ireland, its wild disorders, its loves and hates—all the passionate light and shadow of that fierce and splendid race. . . . Should be read by all those who are interested in this most unusual literary movement of modern times. Indeed they furnish a necessary complement to the over-fanciful pictures drawn by Mr. Yeats of the dim morning of Celtic Song."—*Springfield Republican.*

"Lady Gregory has kept alive the tradition of Ireland as a laughing country. She surpasses the others in the quality of her comedy, however, not that she is more comic, but that she is more comprehensively true to life. Lady Gregory has gone to reality as to a cave of treasure. She is one of the discoverers of Ireland. Her genius, like Synge's, seems to have opened its eyes one day and seen spread below it the immense sea of Irish common speech, with its color, its laughter, and its music."—*Nation.*

G. P. PUTNAM'S SONS

NEW YORK   **LONDON**

Seven Short Plays

By
Lady Gregory
Author of "New Comedies," "Our Irish Theatre," etc.

12⁰.

The plays in this volume are the following: *Spreading the News, Hyacinth Halvey, The Rising of the Moon, The Jackdaw, The Workhouse Ward, The Travelling Man, The Gaol Gate.* The volume also contains music for the songs in the plays and notes explaining the conception of the plays.

Among the three great exponents of the modern Celtic movement in Ireland, Lady Gregory holds an unusual place. It is she from whom came the chief historical impulse which resulted in the re-creation for the present generation of the elemental poetry of early Ireland, its wild disorders, its loves and hates— all the passionate light and shadow of that fierce and splendid race.

G. P. Putnam's Sons
New York   London

Our Irish Theatre

By Lady Gregory

Author of " Irish Folk-History Plays," " New Comedies," etc.

12°.   Illustrated

The volume presents an account not only
of the great contemporary dramatic movement of Ireland, including such names as
those of Synge, Yeats, and Lady Gregory
herself, but of the stage history of the Dublin
Theatre from its erection.   A section of the
book that possesses a very pertinent interest
for American readers is that which has to do
with the bitter antagonism which the Irish
actors encountered on their first visit to our
shores, an antagonism which happily expended
itself and was converted upon the second
visit of these players into approval and enthusiastic endorsement.   The book contains
a full record of the growth and development
of an important dramatic undertaking, in
which the writer has been a directing force.

G. P. Putnam's Sons

New York   **London**